Contents

Native Cultures
of the Pacific Islands

Native Cultures
of the Pacific Islands

DOUGLAS L. OLIVER
Illustrations by Lois Johnson

UNIVERSITY OF HAWAII PRESS

Honolulu

All illustrations have also appeared in *Oceania: The Native Cultures of Australia and the Pacific Islands* (1989, 2 vols., Honolulu: University of Hawaii Press), by Douglas L. Oliver. Source credits are cited in that work.

94 93 92 91 90   5 4 3 2

Library of Congress Cataloging-in-Publication Data

Oliver, Douglas L.
  Native cultures of the Pacific islands.

  Bibliography: p.
  Includes index.
  1. Ethnology—Oceania. 2. Oceania—Social life and
customs. I. Title.
GN662.045   1989   306'.099   88-20625
ISBN 0-8248-1182-8

To Thomas G. Harding
for friendly inducement

Preface

THIS digest, an abridgment of part of a much larger work (*Oceania: The Native Cultures of Australia and the Pacific Islands,* 1989), is about the cultures of the Pacific Islanders as they were before contact with foreigners, mainly Europeans, changed them in extensive and profound ways. However, even the larger work could not do full justice to the cultural diversity that obtained among the thousand or so distinctive peoples spread out over that vast region. Recent references to "the Pacific way" contain more rhetoric than reality. What all or most Pacific Islanders now distinctively share is a heritage of colonialism, and even that has many different forms. And what they had in common before colonialism, such as household-based subsistence economies and kinship unit-based land ownership, was to be found in many non-industrial societies elsewhere.

Nevertheless, some readers (including especially teachers) are likely to focus on broad geographic regions for a long time to come, thereby justifying, practically if not always intellectually, regional surveys like this one.

For the more demanding reader, this book can be fleshed out by consulting the larger work, which also contains many footnotes, maps, pictorial illustrations, and an ample bibliography. In this digest bibliographic sources are listed only for those directly quoted or referred to; for other references the reader should consult the larger work.

The larger work also contains a full list of acknowledgments, but I wish to repeat here my gratitude to the many colleagues around the country, and especially to Dr. Thomas Harding, whose continuing use of my *The Pacific Islands* (1961; new, revised edition, 1989) encouraged me to prepare this book, in at least partial fulfillment of their requests.

CHAPTER ONE

Physical Setting

THE thousand or so distinctive peoples—the Pacific Islanders—whose cultures are summarized in this book inhabited nearly every island north and east of Australia between longitudes 130 E and 110 W, and between latitudes 25 N and 47 S. The boundary we draw between them and the Aborigines of Australia–Tasmania has not always been so sharp: the pioneer immigrants into both New Guinea and Australia stemmed from the same or closely related Southeast Asian peoples, but after many millennia of spatial separation the cultures of their respective descendants had become widely divergent. The distinction made here between the Pacific Islanders and their neighbors in the Moluccas is less defensible, but a line must be drawn somewhere, and this one has some justification in prehistorical terms. Although peoples and culture traits from the Moluccas (and possibly also the southern Philippines) had continued to trickle eastward after their first movements into the Islands 40,000 to 50,000 years ago, for tens of millennia the neolithic and pagan lives of the Pacific Islanders remained largely untouched by the metal technologies and "high civilizations" of Southeast Asia. But before discussing these and other matters having to do with the peopling of the Pacific Islands, let us take a look at the physical setting into which the people moved and in which they learned to survive and proliferate.

The layer of rock, sixty miles or so thick, composing the earth's crust and upper mantle (the lithosphere) floats on a relatively fluid layer of molten magma and is divided into a number of huge, rigid, and constantly moving plates. When adjoining plates move apart, the underlying magma flows up through the gaps to build mountain ridges. Or, when plates collide one of them subducts (pushes under) the other, creating great ridges and troughs. And when they grind past each other the resulting friction produces cracks (transform faults) in the adjoining plates.

The Pacific Islands (as herein identified) are based on three adjoining plates: the vast Pacific Plate in the east (which consists mainly of basalt),

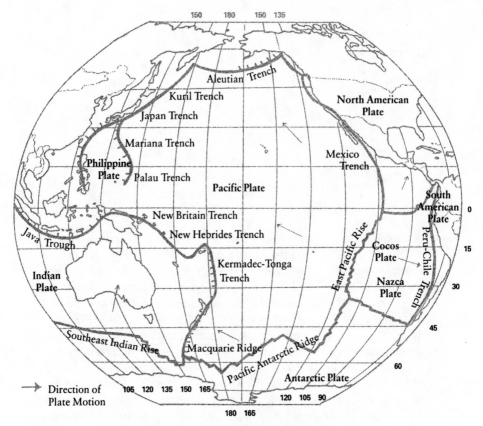

Figure 1.1 Tectonic plates of the Pacific Region
(from *Scientific American,* June 1979:166)

and the Philippine and Indo-Australian plates in the west (which consist of continental-type rocks such as granite and slate) (Fig. 1.1). At its western edge, the westward-drifting Pacific Plate subducts the other two, thereby forming mountainous ridges and deep ocean trenches, accompanied by continuing vulcanism and earthquakes. Meanwhile, the magma underlying the Pacific Plate continues to flow up through its faults, thereby adding to the existing archipelagoes.

Another phenomenon involved in the building of the Pacific Islands in the tropics is the formation of coral, a hard calcareous substance made up of the skeletons of certain marine animals and plants. The animals in question are polyps (coelenterates), which make their own shells by secretion from salt water. During their final life stage, polyps attach themselves to a solid surface, either to rocks or to the shells of dead polyps, and in this way build up solid calcareous structures of diverse shapes. The plants taking part in this process are microscopic algae, which first live within the cells of the polyps and stimulate their calcium metabolism and later fill the dead shells of their hosts with their own calcareous corpses. Coral-forming polyps live and multiply only in warm, saline, and clear sunlit water, which in the Pacific constitutes a belt about thirty degrees wide on both sides of the equator and with depths of less than about 150 feet. Because of these limits, as a coral-encrusted shoreline rises and falls in relation to sea level so does its zone of coral formation. Thus, as a result of the many changes in shoreline level that have occurred in the Pacific over millions of years, dead coral reefs are to be found on the slopes of some islands as much as 4,000 feet above, or below, present sea level. Coral was an important element in the lives of many Pacific Islanders, but it is the shore-level changes them-selves that deserve our immediate interest.

During the Pleistocene there occurred several large worldwide shore-level changes that resulted less from up-and-down movements of the land than from rises and falls of the sea level itself.

The Pleistocene period, which began two to three million years ago, was defined by a series of wide swings in atmospheric temperature. Dur-ing the periods of lowest temperatures, huge ice caps developed in the Northern Hemisphere (and smaller mountaintop ice fields in the South-ern Hemisphere) thereby freezing (impounding) vast quantities of water that would otherwise have served to replenish the water lost from the oceans by normal evaporation. One effect of this impounding was to lower shoreline water levels around the world.

The shore-level changes that had most to do with human history in the Pacific Islands occurred in the southern part of the area stretching from mainland Southeast Asia to the eastern edges of Australia and New Guinea. At various times during the Pleistocene, the sea level in that area dropped so low that previously (and presently) discrete islands were either joined to one another or separated by much narrower channels. These conditions facilitated the spread of terrestrial plants and animals throughout that area, most significantly from west to east. Most cru-cially for the subject matter of this book, the fauna thus affected included humans. The chains of islands stretching from New Guinea to New Cale-donia were also enlarged and brought nearer together by these drops in sea level, and their biota thereby enriched, but less so than the case of New Guinea itself. In the case of islands farther north and east (those now known as Micronesia and Polynesia), their isolation was reduced only slightly, and inconsequently, by the lowering of their shorelines.

Wide shoreline oscillations continued throughout the whole of the Pleistocene, but it was only during the last phase of that period that such changes directly affected the humans with whom this book in concerned. That phase began about 120,000 years ago and "ended" (perhaps tempo-rarily?) with the Holocene, or Recent, geological era, which began about

10,000 years ago and is characterized by the kind of (relative) stability in climate, and hence in worldwide sea levels, that now prevails. Throughout the final phase of the Pleistocene, sea levels were always somewhat lower than they are today, but during two lengthy subphases they reached depths as low as 400–475 feet below present levels. During those subphases, one that reached its climax about 53,000 years ago and the other some 33,000 years later, the land surfaces of the western Pacific looked as shown on Figure 1.2. (The shaded areas are those presently under water but which were exposed by the lowered sea levels of those times.)

As shown in Figure 1.2, two continent-sized land units, Sunda and Sahul, were created by the lowered sea levels. Although they themselves were not connected, the water gaps between them were reduced by enlargement of the islands between them. The dry-land shelf connecting Sunda with mainland Asia made it possible for animals, including humanoid, and later fully human, primates, to walk dry-footed as far east as the eastern shores of Borneo and Java. But to reach from there to Sahul, which the fully human primates achieved no later than about 40,000 to 50,000 years ago, would have required them to cross stretches of ocean at least 36 nautical miles wide. We will consider in chapter 2 who those earliest human settlers in Sahul were, but let us look now at the kinds of natural environments they found when they stepped ashore there.

That, of course, would have depended upon the location of their landfall, or rather landfalls: it is reasonable to assume that the crossings were made by several different groups and that two or more routes were followed. Those following the northern routes would have landed on the relatively narrow shores fringing New Guinea (which is mountainous in that part), and those taking the central and southern routes onto the flat shelflands, now under water, that extended for hundreds of miles out from Australia's present northwestern shoreline.

Until about 10,000 years ago, when it became much as it is today, the climate of the late Pleistocene phase was more humid than at present in all those landfall areas, and although somewhat cooler than today's it was still warm enough to be labeled "tropical." (At that time, however, glaciers existed in the mountains of southeast Australia and central New Guinea.) But long before the present-day climates had become established, the descendants of the earlier groups of human immigrants had pushed much farther east and south. By about 25,000 years ago, they had penetrated deep into the mountainous interior of New Guinea, some 900–1,000 miles east of the original landfalls. (And by 30,000 years ago they had moved down Australia's eastern side at least as far as the site of present Melbourne.)

Figure 1.2 Sunda and Sahul (shaded areas now submerged)

The earlier pioneers in Australia and New Guinea (which were at that time united) found vegetation very similar to the kinds they had left behind in Sunda, including most of those kinds of plants collected for food. The same may be said of some species of animals, except for several mammals (e.g., elephants, rhinos, monkeys, and apes) that never managed to reach Sahul. In compensation, the pioneer settlers in Sahul found several unfamiliar animals, including giant flightless birds (e.g., emus and cassowaries) and marsupials, some of which were larger than any now alive (e.g., nine-foot-tall kangaroos; giant, wombat-like Diprotodons; and leopard-sized marsupial "lions").

We turn now to the topography, climate, and other features of the Pacific Islands during the Recent era, when they came to be as they now are, about 10,000 years ago. Geologically, the Islands may be divided into several types.

Continental islands are those formed by processes of sedimentation, folding, faulting, and so forth and, thus, consisting mainly of continental-type rocks. Such islands also contain intrusions of volcanic rock and have their shorelines encrusted with live and dead coral, and their heterogeneous foundations provide them with wider variations of profiles and soils than can be found on other types of Pacific Islands. All the continental islands are located on the Philippine and Indo-Australian plates; examples of them include New Zealand, Viti Levu, New Caledonia, Guadalcanal, and New Guinea.

Volcanic islands are those formed mainly by volcanic intrusion on all three of the plates (e.g., Manam, Kolombangara, Upolu, Tahiti, Oahu, and Ponape). Compared with those of the continental islands, the basic rocks of the volcanic islands are quite homogeneous, consisting chiefly of volcanic products, but the islands themselves differ widely in shape, due mainly to differences in weathering and in the kind of volcanic intrusion (either explosive or flow-type) that formed them. Thus, the Hawaiian Archipelago as a whole is more weathered than the Marquesas, and within the former the westernmost and geologically oldest island, Kauai, is more weathered than the island of Hawaii (which is the easternmost, youngest, and in fact still-growing island in the chain). The ultimate in weathering is represented by those islands whose presence above sea level is revealed only by caps of coral.

Coral islands, as described earlier, have been formed by corals throughout the Pacific where the seawater conditions were favorable. Corals mostly occur as reefs off the exposed sides of islands, both continental and volcanic; in many cases they constitute the largest or the only visible parts of such islands. As was noted, the coral deposits of the Pacific vary immensely in depth, and they intergrade continuously in visible (i.e., above sea level) form, from low and narrow atoll islets such as those of Kwajalein, to high and flat-topped ("pancake") islands such as Banaba and Nauru.

One could go on endlessly proposing schemes for classifying the Pacific Islands according to their composition, size, shape, and other features, and inevitably end up with categories that must be labeled "mixed" (such as Truk). But let us move on to some other aspects of the physical

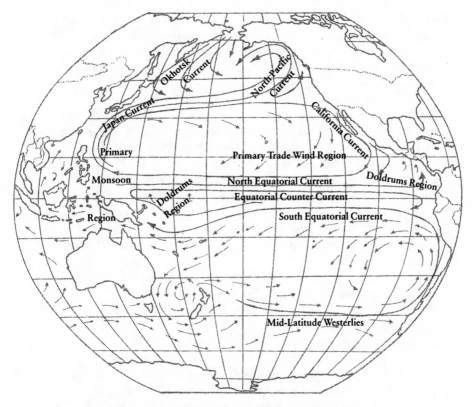

Figure 1.3. Ocean currents and surface winds

environments of the Islands: first, to the major ocean currents that sweep their shores and have affected, directly or indirectly, the lives of their inhabitants.

Two vast whorls dominate water movements in the Pacific (Fig. 1.3). The one north of the equator flows clockwise, its counterpart south of the equator counterclockwise. The southern segment of the northern whorl flows from the American side to the Philippines before it is turned north, except east of the Hawaiian and the Mariana islands, where parts of it are deflected from its east–west course. Some of the northern segment of the southern, westward-moving whorl also flows unobstructed as far as Australia, but much of it is deflected southward by the numerous intervening islands. In between the two major whorls flows the Equatorial Countercurrent in a Pacific-wide band from the Caroline and Gilbert islands all the way to Panama. The width of this band varies between five and ten degrees, and its position shifts northward and southward in concert with the seasonal inclination of the earth.

Islanders living in places brushed by the major currents were influenced by them in two ways. Indirectly, the currents served to determine what species of ocean-borne plants and animals an island received from elsewhere. More directly, they served to facilitate, or to impede, boat travel between islands, with all the cultural and social consequences that such interactions made possible.

Apart from New Zealand, nearly all of the inhabited islands are within the tropics; the other exceptions are Chatham, Raivavae, Rapa, Pitcairn, and Easter. The year-round temperatures experienced in the tropical islands are predictably high. However, surrounded as they are by the ocean, which radiates its stored heat more slowly than do large land areas, few places among these islands experience the very high temperatures that occur in summer in many places in the Temperate Zone. Also, the temperatures in many of the Pacific islands are tempered by offshore winds. And although most of those tropical islands undergo some seasonal change in climate, this results mainly from changes in wind and rainfall.

Surface wind patterns around the Islands are few in number and fairly regular in occurrence (Fig. 1.3). North of about latitude 25 N and south of about latitude 27 S the strong mid-latitude Westerlies blow almost continuously year round. Between them prevail four kinds of wind patterns: trades, monsoons, doldrums, and typhoons.

Trade winds dominate the eastern parts of the tropical Pacific. Those north of the equator blow from the northeast and are strongly felt as far west as about longitude 165 W; those south of it blow from the southeast and spend their main force before reaching as far west. The Pacific trades blow in every month of the year but do so more uninterruptedly and steadily during the period from May to September.

More seasonal winds, or monsoons, take the place of the trades in the western third of the Pacific. The periodic heating and cooling of the Asian land mass, augmented by seasonal changes in Australia, exercise a powerful influence upon wind direction as far east as the Solomons, and some smaller but perceptible influence even farther east. During the Asian winter, winds are pushed out from there to the south and east; the direction is reversed during Asia's summer months. During the Asian winter, the winds, which in the western Pacific become the Northwest Monsoon, are more variable and sometimes stormier than the winds from the east and tend to bring more rain.

The largest areas of doldrums are located between the two trade-wind zones and extend as far west as the Solomons (where the monsoonal pattern takes over). As their name implies, doldrums are characterized by low wind velocities; they are also marked by high humidity, much cloudiness, and by even, year-round high temperatures.

Typhoons (hurricanes) occur throughout much of the tropical Pacific. The high winds and torrential rains that constitute typhoons are devas-

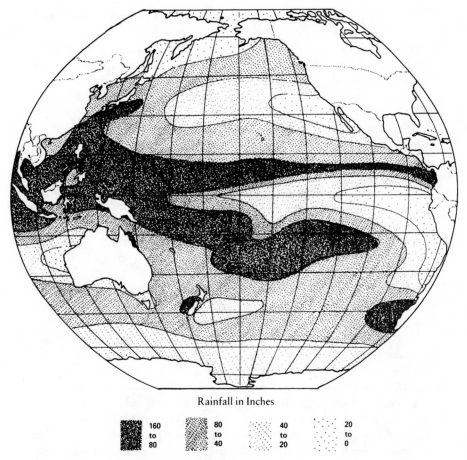

Rainfall in Inches

| 160 to 80 | 80 to 40 | 40 to 20 | 20 to 0 |

Figure 1.4. Rainfall patterns

tating and life-destroying even in our modern era of advance-warning communications and massive rescue operations; they doubtless destroyed whole Island peoples in the past. Like explosive-type volcanic eruptions and unheralded tsunamis (tidal waves), they were an unavoidable hazard to many Pacific Island peoples.

Rainfall in the Pacific Islands is marked by wide variability (Fig. 1.4). Generally speaking, most islands near the equator experience year-round high rainfall, averaging 80–160 inches annually; the islands farther north and south receive about half that amount and on a more seasonal basis. On the other hand, there are several equatorial islands in the central and eastern Pacific that receive virtually no rainfall at all (e.g., Canton, Enderbury), and some others (e.g., southern Gilberts) that receive no rainfall for months at a time. Farther west, where monsoonal winds take over, the rainfall follows a more regular, seasonal pattern, complicated, however, by some islands' mountainous terrain.

Precipitation may also vary among islands in the same archipelago; a prime example of this is in the Hawaiian chain, where Kauai has an annual rainfall in some locations reaching over 600 inches, in contrast to Kahoolawe, which lies in the rainfall "shadow" of Maui and has an average of only 10–25 inches of rainfall a year.

A very widespread pattern of rainfall occurs on those mountainous islands that are located in zones of prevailing, rain-laden winds. Very commonly, such winds drop most of their moisture on the windward slopes, leaving the leeward sides of the islands relatively dry.

The factors, some of them interdependent, most influential in determining the kinds and location of vegetation in the tropical islands of the Pacific were distance from Asia (and, secondarily, from Australia), rainfall, soil (including groundwater level and salinity), altitude (translated into atmospheric temperature), insolation (amount of sunlight), and the actions of humans.

Parts of southern New Guinea share several kinds of indigenous plants with Australia (a heritage, in part, of their union during the Pleistocene), but most of the genera of plants in the tropical Pacific Islands derived from Asia. Concomitantly, and other factors being equal, the farther from Asia an island is, the fewer genera of plants it will contain, a tendency greatly increased by the progressively wider water gaps, from west to east, separating the islands from Asia. In other words, the only plants that managed to migrate into such islands were those whose reproductive parts could be carried by wind or birds (or later by man) or those that could survive long immersion in seawater. Thus, plants "dropped out" in the journey from west to east so that, for example, although Bougainville Island in the Solomons contained hundreds of genera of pre-European plants, Easter Island (about 6,500 miles to the southeast) contained only about thirty *species*. The "other factors" referred to earlier served to modify this pattern somewhat (e.g., Canton, a true "desert" island, is much less isolated and is nearer to Asia than are the high volcanic islands of the Marquesas but contains fewer genera of plants than the latter), but the distance-from-Asia pattern generally does hold true.

A few plants had migrated successfully to the Pacific Islands from the Americas in pre-European times, but compared with contributions from Asia and even Australia the numbers from the eastern direction have been small and very limited in distribution, except for the sweet potato, which will be discussed in chapter 3.

The thinning out of plant genera from west to east seems not to have been balanced by the development of much endemism in the Islands at the genus level. On the other hand, on many islands some of the genera have evolved into profusions of distinct species.

In pre-European times the major changes wrought by humans in the natural environments of the Islands came about as results of gardening and hunting, whereby some fairly extensive areas were cleared or burnt over and converted eventually either to secondary forest or grassland or scrub, or more or less permanent clearings for habitation and gardening. Such changes aside, it will be useful to list the major types of pristine plant associations encountered by humans when they first settled the Islands.

Seacoast or strand. This complex, which is present on nearly every tropical Pacific Island, and indeed throughout insular Southeast Asia as well, is usually confined to very narrow areas and contains only a small number of genera. The larger tree-sized plants usually include casuarina (ironwood), barringtonia, hibiscus, pandanus, and Indian almond. With these are usually found the white-flowered scaevola shrub, various woody vines and legumes, wiry bunchgrass, sedges, and the extremely useful coconut palm (which, however, is found mainly where it has been planted by man). Common to all these plants is the capacity to thrive in salt or brackish water; in fact, they owe their wide distribution to the ability of their seeds to be borne long distances in the ocean without loss of viability.

Mangrove forests. This complex includes "true" mangrove trees, terrestrial ferns, and epiphytes (air plants); in other words, plants specially adapted to growth in mud flats partly or totally covered by salt or brackish water. Such plants thrive along shores protected from wind and wave and along the swampy banks of tidal creeks. Trees of the mangrove genus *(Rhizophora)* have slender but very tough trunks and are supported by numerous prop roots. They serve to collect alluvium, hence to extend shores outward, but beyond that seem to have had little or no utility for the Pacific Islanders.

Swamps. Several types of swamp vegetation occur in the Islands, either in large and pure stands (as, for example, along the course of the Sepik River in New Guinea) or interspersed among other complexes, including some at very high altitudes. In a few places of relatively dense population, the swamps were drained for gardening; in other places their sago palms were harvested for food; in most others they were left entirely alone.

Lowland rainforest. Throughout the "continental" lands of the western islands and on most of the mountainous volcanic islands of the central and eastern Pacific this was the most widespread type of vegetation complex, and one divisible into many subtypes. Forests of this type are characterized by large numbers of different plants, including huge trees festooned with vines and ferns.

Montane or subtropical rainforest. Under similar conditions of atmospheric moisture, the vegetation of the lowland rainforest is replaced by other species on lands of higher altitude or greater distance from the equator, or both. The plants of this complex differ somewhat from island to island but in general consist of only two levels of vegetation, in place of the three to five found in their lowland counterparts.

High montane cloud forest. In New Guinea this complex replaces the montane rainforest at about 6,000 feet; in other islands where it is found (which are not many) the transition from rainforest to cloud forest takes place at lower altitudes. In this chill, wet atmosphere there is generally a single-story canopy, and the dominant trees are temperate-zone ones such as myrtles and rhododendrons, festooned with mosses and liverworts and ornamented with orchids.

Alpine vegetation. Above the usual cloud level the climates of the highest tropical islands become dry and sunny, and the mossy forests change, first into shrubby woodland and higher still into tussocky grasses and herbs. Patches of such vegetation occur at the summits of the highest mountains in the Solomons, but large indigenous stands of this kind of vegetation occur only in New Guinea and in the Hawaiian chain.

Grasslands and savannah woodland. Vegetation complexes of this type now occur widely in the Pacific Islands, either indigenously, as a result of insufficient rainfall, or as a result of continuous burning of the original forest by humans. The largest of these areas are on New Guinea (e.g., in the Highlands and south of the Fly River). Smaller stretches are located on the leeward sides of some large islands, such as Guadalcanal, New Caledonia, Viti Levu, and the island of Hawaii. And even smaller, but nevertheless extensive, stretches of it occur on Easter Island and on some other islands of the Hawaiian chain.

And finally, there is New Zealand. The two principal islands of this archipelago extend north and south some 745 miles and comprise about 96,000 square miles of land, which is larger than the total of all the other islands occupied by Polynesian-speaking peoples in pre-European times. Even the northernmost tip of New Zealand, at latitude 34 S, is well outside the tropics, and the southern tip of the archipelago's South Island is only 23 degrees from the Antarctic Circle, all of which resulted in a variety of climates (and of vegetation) ranging from semitropical (where four-fifths of its indigenous people lived) to one too cold to permit its thin scattering of them to garden.

Turning now to the indigenous animals of the Islands, four factors influenced what kinds of vertebrates lived there and where they lived. One has been the unbridged ocean gaps between the Islands and Asia during the last sixty or so million years, which accounts for the absence in the Islands of the larger vertebrates of Asia. Another factor was the dry-land connection between Australia and New Guinea during some phases of the Pleistocene, which resulted in their having many vertebrates, especially marsupials and flightless birds, in common. A third has been the vast distances between the easternmost islands and the nearest American shores, and, consequently, their total lack of any common terrestrial vertebrates. And the fourth factor has been the progressively wider ocean distances between the island archipelagoes from west to east, which resulted in a corresponding attenuation of terrestrial vertebrate genera. Thus, although New Guinea contains 72 genera of indigenous mammals, Bougainville Island has only 15, and the easternmost archipelagoes have only rodents (and even those may have been introduced, unwittingly, in Islanders' canoes). Moreover, the same west-to-east attenuation prevailed for other land-living vertebrates, including birds (of which New Guinea contained 860 species and Tahiti only 17). Even New Zealand was affected by this factor with respect to, say, mammals and reptiles (but not with respect to its many species of flightless birds, which may have been faunal remnants of New Zealand's land connection with Australia tens of millions of years ago).

Distance, of course, was not an absolute obstacle to the truly oceanic birds (such as gulls, terns, noddies, albatrosses, and shearwaters), nor to some far-flying land birds such as the golden plover (which migrates annually from Alaska to Hawaii and beyond). And although freshwater fauna tended to be influenced by the same rule of distance that governed terrestrial fauna, the distribution of saltwater fauna was determined by conditions of other kinds, including currents, water temperature, undersea topography, and coral formation.

Finally, mention must be made of two other organisms that affected many Pacific Islanders in very important ways. One was the malaria-bearing anopheles mosquito, which infested most islands from New Guinea to, but not including, New Caledonia. The other was the filaria-bearing mosquito, *Aedes polynesiensis,* which infested a chain of islands stretching from New Guinea to eastern Polynesia.

Sources

Allen, Golson, and Jones 1977; Kay 1980; Thomas 1968.

CHAPTER TWO
Prehistory

ATTEMPTS to synthesize data bearing on mankind's prehistory should be written on erasable bond. This is especially true of the Pacific Islands, where new discoveries are continually accelerating. It fact, it can be predicted with near certainty that during the interval between writing this chapter and having it appear in print many of its minor and perhaps some of its major conclusions will have to be abandoned or revised. Nevertheless, an attempt should be made, however tentative its conclusions, to propose connections between the different kinds of data: somatological, linguistic, and artifactual.

I begin by conjecturing that during and perhaps even before the period from about 60,000 to 8,000 years ago the Islands immediately to the west of New Guinea were inhabited by thinly scattered bands of dark-skinned humans with curly to frizzly hair of two distinct physical types: one that was fully "modern" (type T), and another, type S, that contained more genetic heritage from the earlier, more "primitive" Erectine inhabitants of the area (which included the well-known *Pithecanthropus erectus*). The precise geographical distribution of types T and S is debatable: they were either segregated into separate bands (and separate inbreeding populations), or mixed together in all or most bands, or distributed, intra- and interband, along a west-to-east cline.

In any case, all of these Sundanoids (as I shall label them) lived by hunting and gathering. Most of their tools were probably fashioned out of wood, shell, antler, and bone, but they also made stone tools, for direct use and for fashioning and maintaining the nonlithic ones. Their earliest stone tools consisted of unretouched flakes and of chopping tools (a heritage of the earlier Erectines?), but these were eventually superceded, around 15,000 to 12,000 years ago, by retouched flakes and edge-ground axes and adzes. It is plausible (but unprovable) to suggest that the languages spoken by the Sundanoids included some that were ancestral to those that have come to be labeled Australian and Papuan.

Then, beginning at least 40,000 years ago and possibly as early as thirteen millennia before that (when the sea level was at a very low margin), some Sundanoids crossed the several remaining water gaps separating Sunda from Sahul. Different groups of migrants probably followed different routes and landed at many different places, from the northwestern capes of New Guinea to the Sahul Shelf of Australia, along an arc about 2,000 miles long. And they continued such movements, off and on, for many millennia more, until, in fact, they were superceded thousands of years later by peoples of Mongoloid physical type (some of whom have continued to cross into the Pacific Islands ever since).

On the evidence of early skeletal remains in Australia, both S- and T-type Sundanoids reached that continent and remained segregated from one another, genetically, for many millennia. By about 5,000 years ago, the two types had partly merged throughout most of Australia, although the T type continued to predominate in the north and the S type in the south, except in Tasmania, whose pioneer T-type population escaped that merging as a result of the re-flooding of the Bass Strait (between Tasmania and the mainland) 7,000 to 8,000 years ago.

Human skeletal remains older than about 5,000 years have not yet been found in New Guinea, but on the evidence of present-day and recently deceased populations there, the first (i.e., Sundanoid) settlers on the island had more T- than S-type genes. However, in comparison with Australia, where the terrain contained few physical barriers, the early New Guinea peoples remained or became more distinct from one another, genetically, for many millennia, long enough, in fact, to reinforce or develop wide diversities in physical types.

These genetic events had their parallels in linguistic prehistory.

The 300 or so languages being spoken by the Aborigines of Australia when Europeans arrived there two centuries ago were extremely diverse but possessed enough common features to suggest that they had derived from several closely related families of languages. (The languages of the nineteenth-century Tasmanians differed more widely from those of the mainland, a consequence of their 7,000-year separation from the latter, but there is no evidence that their ancestral languages were *not* members of some mainland language families.)

Two fundamentally different kinds of languages were (and still are) spoken on New Guinea: one labeled Papuan, the other Austronesian. Beginning with the former, it has been proposed by some linguists that most of the 720 or so of them are "genetically" interrelated, although the argument for their ancestral unity is less conclusive than in the case of the proposed unity of their Australian counterparts. Moreover, a few of the languages labeled Papuan have so far resisted efforts to link them with the rest, or with any other languages elsewhere. These exceptions aside, the main body of Papuan languages is believed by some linguists to be the "descendants" of those spoken by four separate streams of immigrants from the west (most of whom, it can be plausibly conjectured, were Sundanoid in physical type). Included in the linguists' reconstruction is the proposal that the peoples speaking the last of the four "streams" of Papuan languages entered western New Guinea about 10,000 years ago, via Timor-Alor-Pantai, after which their descendants pushed eastward nearly to the island's eastern shores, absorbing or eliminating most other peoples met with on the way. Then, this theory continues, about 5,000 years ago speakers of these fourth-stream languages living in the Markham River valley of New Guinea made contact with newly arrived Austronesian speakers, and the resulting stimulus moved them to resume their migrations, this time back through New Guinea and all the way to the Moluccas again. The authors of this reconstruction go on to say that the languages "descended" from those spoken by the fourth-stream migrants now constitute a fairly homogeneous group, called the Trans-New Guinea phylum, whose present-day speakers comprise over eighty percent of all Papuan-speakers and who occupy most of the interior of New Guinea (and parts of the Moluccas as well).

It may have been pressure from the fourth-stream migrations that dislodged speakers of an earlier East Papuan phylum stream of languages and sent them to New Britain, Bougainville, and on down the chain of islands as far south as Santa Cruz, although it is possible that this movement began voluntarily, at earlier (or later) dates.

In view of the indubitable horticultural technology of the Austronesian speakers with whom the Markham Valley Papuans had contact, it is reasonable to believe that the movement of the latter back, westward, through the island carried along some elements of that technology. But it is also tempting to link the initial extensive and evidently unstoppable eastern progress of those fourth-stream Sundanoids with an even earlier diffusion of horticulture into New Guinea. Support for this suggestion comes from the Central Highlands of New Guinea, where indirect signs of gardening and pig domestication have been found at archaeological sites dated about 9,000 years ago (i.e., about 1,000 years after the linguists' date for the arrival of the Trans-New Guinea language-speakers on the island's western shores). These signs of horticulture predate any others so far discovered in Southeast Asia, but the Highlands data cannot be ignored, and their possible linkage with the Trans-New Guinea language-speakers cannot be entirely dismissed.

I also offer, in the spirit of adventurous speculation, the suggestion that the refined lithic technology (consisting of ground ax–adzes of lenticular cross section) uncovered in New Guinea's Central Highlands, and also dated circa 9,000 years ago, may also be attributed to those enterprising Trans-New Guinea phylum-speakers. (Possible prototypes of such tools have been found in Southeast Asia and Australia in sites

20,000 and more years old, but the type referred to here is much more refined than those.)

And finally, the appearance in the Highlands at about this time of marine shells (from coasts at least 100 miles away) implies a quickened movement of peoples and objects, in keeping with those attributed to the fast-spreading Trans-New Guinea phylum-speakers.

At some times between 10,000 and 5,000 years ago, four epochal innovations entered the Pacific Islands from the west: (1) genes carrying Mongoloid (in contrast to Sundanoid) physical traits, (2) some languages of the Austronesian family, (3) some ideas and objects relating to plant cultivation and animal domestication, and (4) some marked improvements in boats and boat handling. This period also witnessed the entry into the Islands of several other important kinds of cultural innovations from the west (e.g., quadrangular stone adzes, pottery making, new forms of social organization, and new religious ideas and practices), but these were in a sense accessory to the four itemized.

It was conjectured above about the newcomers' physical traits that the first human migrants into the Islands, specifically into New Guinea, were Sundanoid (peoples with dark skins and curly to frizzly hair). Evidence for this conjecture is largely circuitous; for example, most present-day indigenes of the interior of New Guinea are Sundanoid, as are (and were) the aboriginal peoples of the islands immediately to the west. However, that conjecture, as worded, is not very informative; it says nothing about the stature or cranial shapes or facial forms of the peoples referred to, nor about any other of the many physical traits that bear witness to a population's genetic makeup. Unfortunately, evidence bearing on those criteria is also circuitous, depending as it does upon characteristics of New Guinea's present peoples and on ancient skeletal remains found in Australia and Southeast Asia (no human skeletal remains have been found on New Guinea older than about 5,000 years). Nevertheless, circuitous or not, such evidence is all we have, and in the absence of contrary evidence, the "Sundanoid connection" makes good sense.

The Sundanoid colonists in New Guinea eventually occupied most of that huge island, as well as most of the larger islands farther east and southeast as far as New Caledonia (which was first settled by about 4,000 years ago). In the course of the many millennia required for all these movements, the many separate bands of migrating Sundanoids evolved into numerous pockets of distinctive physical types, in consequence of their mutual isolations over very long periods of time, isolations fostered by geographic barriers and reinforced by attitudes of ethnocentricity (which, by the way, continued to prevail until modern times).

Meanwhile, on the northern side of the Sundanoid domain, and on into eastern and northeastern Asia, lived peoples of markedly different (i.e., Mongoloid) physical traits (e.g., lighter color of skin, straighter hair, rounder crania, flatter brow ridges). Experts disagree regarding the original connection between Sundanoids and Mongoloids. Some view them as having evolved separately from entirely different precursors and as having remained separate for a long time thereafter. Others view them as having always constituted a cline, with the most Mongoloid-type peoples living at the northern end of the cline and the most Sundanoid-type peoples at the southeastern end, with the two types shading into one another in between. Whatever the actuality (knowledge of which must await the discovery of more skeletal evidence from the vast arc between the ends), by about 5,000 years ago peoples with distinctly Mongoloid genes seem to have settled far beyond their original homelands and to have replaced (either supplanted or absorbed) most of the Sundanoid peoples remaining in southeast Asia. (Most, but not all: pockets of the latter are still found in Malaya [i.e., the Semang], in the Philippines [the so-called Negritos], in the Moluccas, and in the Andamans.)

Then, beginning about 5,500 years ago peoples with Mongoloid genes began moving into the Pacific Islands, either in the form of "pure" Mongoloids, or of Mongoloid-Sundanoid hybrids. Early in that era some peoples of mainly Mongoloid type made the long over-water journey into western Micronesia (at least 3,600 years ago, according to artifacts discovered in the Marianas). And at about the same time another group, or set of closely interrelated groups, of more or less Mongoloid peoples initiated a series of eastward, relatively fast-moving migrations along or directly north of New Guinea's northern coast and thence through the Solomons and New Hebrides and beyond.

At this point a reminder is in order. The physical category of Mongoloid just referred to includes a wide range of physical types, from the light-skinned, straight-haired, medium-statured, round-headed, flat-faced peoples of northern China, Korea, and eastern Siberia, to the many brown-skinned, wavy haired, short-statured, narrow-headed, more sharp-faced present-day peoples of Indonesia and the Philippines. (Plus, of course, the American Indians, who are also widely diverse but basically Mongoloid.) The specific populations from which the Mongoloids of the Pacific Islands originally derived probably came from the southeastern, coastal parts of the Mongoloid cline but not all from the same populations. Hence, they were not all exactly the same in physical type. (As is the case of the Sundanoids, the Mongoloid populations themselves are characterized by some intra-populational diversity.)

The migrations just described served to introduce members of a family of languages, now called Austronesian, which differ from the Papuan languages in several fundamental respects. There are now some 700–800 Austronesian languages, spoken by more than 150 million people, living from mainland Southeast Asia and Formosa to Hawaii and Easter Island, with an offshoot in Madagascar as well. The languages ancestral to mod-

Figure 2.1. Major divisions of the Austronesian language family

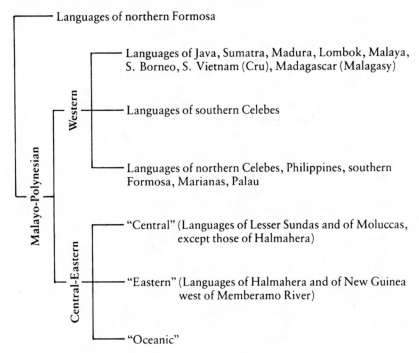

ern-day Austronesian languages are likely to have originated in South China or Formosa, or both, and the first major division among them took place about 6,000 years ago. When that occurred, one branch of the family was carried to (or remained in?) Formosa, and the other, now known as the Malayo-Polynesian branch, spread out to the south and eventually divided in the ways shown in Figure 2.1. Of the present-day Austronesian languages of the Pacific Islands, those of the Mariana and Palau islands have been consigned to the Western branch of Malayo-Polynesian, and those of Yap and Nauru, although undeniably Austronesian, have not yet been more specifically classified, but all the others are included in the Oceanic branch. Because of its direct bearing upon the Islanders' prehistory, I reproduce in Figure 2.2 an authoritative diagram of the complex branching of this Oceanic division, which began about 5,000 years ago.

Two features of Figures 2.1 and 2.2 are especially noteworthy. First is the indication that the languages of the Palau and Mariana islands (and of Yap and Nauru) are, although Austronesian, only distantly related to those of the Oceanic division. Second is the large number and the far-flung distribution (evidently due to rapid branching) of the Hebridean–Central Pacific subdivision, particularly of its Polynesian branch.

In the absence of dissonant evidence, it is certain that the pioneers who

Figure 2.2. A tentative family tree for the Oceanic languages (after Bellwood 1979:125)

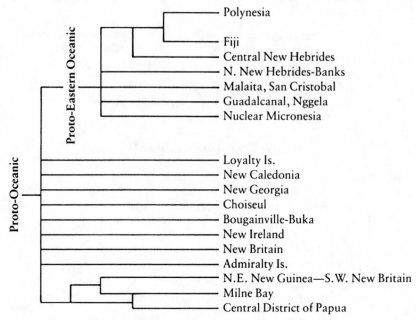

introduced Austronesian languages into Palau and the Marianas (and probably into Yap and Nauru) were mainly Mongoloid in physical type. That was also true of the pioneer migrants into the Gilbert, Marshall, and other Caroline islands, and of those who populated much of Polynesia. Also, in most of present-day New Guinea and in parts of the Solomons, the peoples who speak Papuan languages are decidedly Sundanoid in physical type. Elsewhere in the Islands, however, the linkage between physical type and language is not so close. Many of the coastal and off-shore-island peoples of New Guinea, and most of those of the rest of Melanesia, of Fiji, and even of parts of Polynesia are dark-skinned and curly to frizzly haired, yet spoke Austronesian languages, which demonstrates that the new (i.e., Mongoloid) genes and the new (Austronesian) speech patterns in the Islands did not always travel together or remain together ever after.

The same may be said of many other cultural traits, including horticulture and animal domestication.

As noted earlier, archaeological evidence suggests the presence of gardening and pigs (possibly domesticated) in the Central Highlands of New Guinea as early as 9,000 years ago. Even if so early an occurrence turns out to be untrue, it seems likely that ideas about producing food, as contrasted with hunting and gathering it, had spread from the west into New

Guinea some time before the actual arrival of any Austronesian-speaking and Mongoloid-looking peoples (who certainly also carried such ideas with them). Moreover, it is also likely that some actual cultivable plants, and some domesticable animals had arrived in New Guinea, unaccompanied by peoples of Mongoloid physical type and of Austronesian speech.

The fourth, and crucially important, set of innovations to enter the Island domain about 5,000 years ago was some marked improvements in the form of and handling of boats, which facilitated, or in many cases was indispensable for, spread of the other innovations just described.

To the descendants of the Sundanoid peoples who had managed to cross the water gaps separating Sunda from Sahul, the crossings from eastern New Guinea to New Britain and thence to New Ireland, to Nissan, to Buka–Bougainville, and on down the Solomon chain to San Cristobal would have presented no insuperable difficulties. No minimal interisland distance along that route would have exceeded forty statute miles, and the high profiles of nearly all of the intervening islands would have provided visible encouragement most of the way. This was not so from San Cristobal onwards. From there, the next landfalls would have been Ndeni Island (230 miles to the east) and tiny Torres Island (325 miles to the southeast). After that, shorter stages led on to the New Hebrides and New Caledonia; between Ndeni or Torres Island to Fiji, however, there is open water for about 525 miles.

In other words, although simpler craft (say, large rafts or simple dugout canoes) may have been capable of transporting people as far south and east as San Cristobal, more seaworthy craft, or miracles of human endurance, would have been required to settle the islands beyond there. Craft of the type required may, perhaps, have been invented in the Islands themselves, but on the basis of evidence too detailed to consider here, it is much more likely that the basic innovation in this technology (i.e., the addition of an outrigger balance to a single-hull canoe) was made in eastern or Southeast Asia, whence it first diffused into the Pacific Islands, with or without its inventors, beginning about 4,000 to 5,000 years ago.

Similarly, the pioneer migrations into Palau and the Marianas, which occurred no later than about 3,600 years ago and which seem to have originated in lands bordering the Celebes Sea, would have required boats capable of crossing open-ocean distances of no less than 450–500 miles.

To proceed much further in this attempt to outline man's prehistory in the Pacific Islands is to incur revision even before the printer's ink of the published book is dry. Evidence bearing on genetic (i.e., racial) relationships is so patchy, or so ambiguous, or (in the case of present-day populations) so clouded by recent interbreeding, that there are almost as many theories as theorists. There is considerably more consensus among linguists concerning relationships among most individual languages in

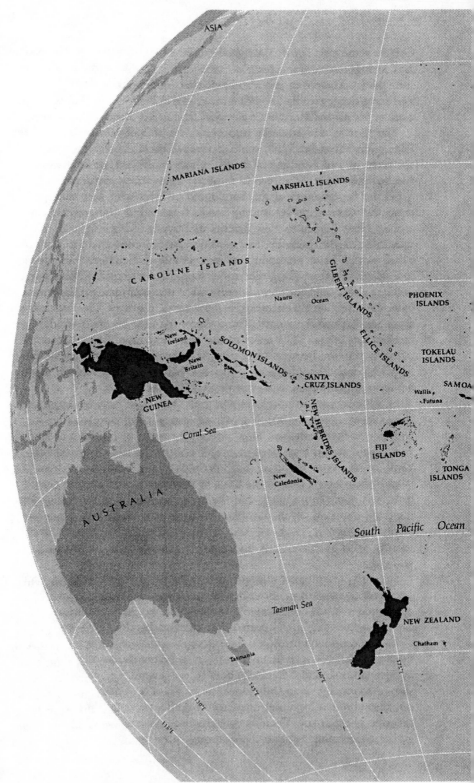

Figure 2.3. The Pacific

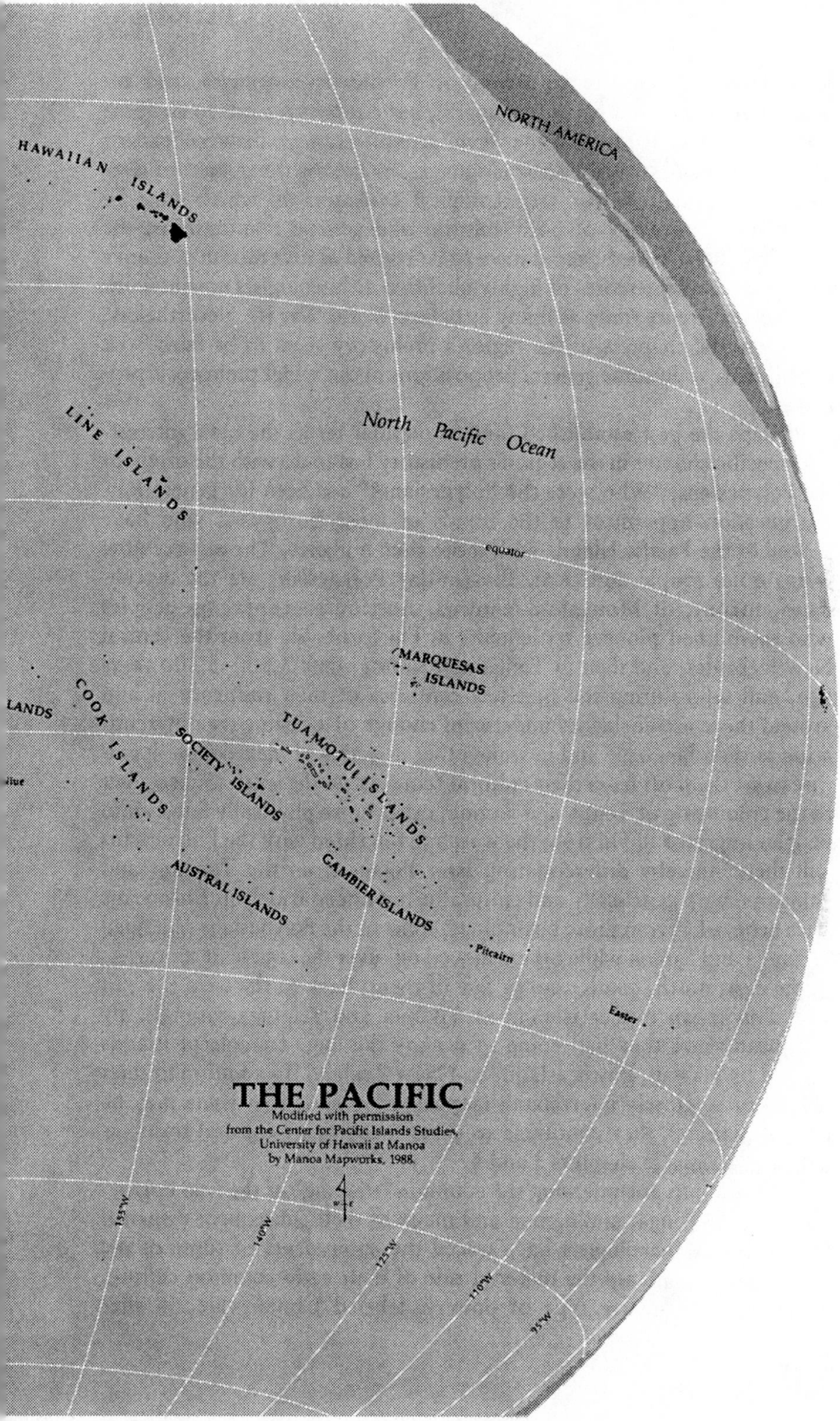

NORTH AMERICA

HAWAIIAN ISLANDS

LINE ISLANDS

North Pacific Ocean

equator

MARQUESAS ISLANDS

LANDS

COOK ISLANDS

SOCIETY ISLANDS

TUAMOTU ISLANDS

iue

AUSTRAL ISLANDS

GAMBIER ISLANDS

• Pitcairn

Easter •

THE PACIFIC
Modified with permission
from the Center for Pacific Islands Studies,
University of Hawaii at Manoa
by Manoa Mapworks, 1988.

145°W

135°W

125°W

115°W

95°W

lower-level groupings (e.g., among all Polynesian languages, and between Polynesian and Fijian languages), but consensus tends to decrease with schemes concerning higher-level groupings (e.g., between eastern Micronesian and central Pacific languages, or among the numerous divisions of Papuan). As for archaeological evidence, on which must be based the chronology of both cultural and genetic relationships, the reconstructions gained from it have to be revised almost monthly, thanks to the efforts of the scores of highly qualified archaeologists now at work (i.e., ten or twenty times as many as before World War II). Nevertheless, a few specific chapters of the region's prehistory seem to be fairly well established, as do some general propositions about wider prehistoric processes.

Perhaps the best established (and in popular terms the most interesting) specific chapter in the region's prehistory has to do with the origin of the Polynesians. "Who were the Polynesians?" has been for generations the question uppermost in the minds of most Europeans who have looked at the Pacific Islands with more than a glance. The answer now seems quite simple and clear. Present-day Polynesians are the descendants, mainly, of Mongoloid-featured, Austronesian-speaking peoples who established pioneer settlements in Fiji (probably from the central New Hebrides) and then in Tonga and Samoa some 3,500–3,300 years ago, and who during the first few centuries of their residence in and around those archipelagoes underwent enough of a distinctive differentiation in their language and in some other domains of their common culture to set them off from their cultural "cousins" in the west. (Subsequent to the colonizing of Tonga and Samoa, other more physically Sundanoid peoples migrated to Fiji from the west and interbred with the Polynesians still there, thereby differentiating later Fijians from the Tongans and Samoans, both genetically and culturally, but not so widely as Europeans once believed.) From those beginnings, some of the Polynesians remained in Tonga and Samoa while others moved on, over the course of centuries, to the east, north, south, and (a few of them) back to the west (i.e., to such Polynesian outlier islands as Tikopia and Kapingamarangi). By European times they had come to occupy the huge triangle of islands formed by Hawaii, Easter Island, and New Zealand. In addition to their twenty or so closely interrelated languages (so close that some may be labeled dialects), they continued to share many other cultural traits, as will be described in chapters 3 and 4.

In addition to documenting the common "shaping" of the first Polynesians in Fiji, Tonga, and Samoa and much of their subsequent dispersal from there, archaeologists have traced the antecedents of some of the artifacts that made up the material side of their early common culture, including a distinctive type of pottery, labeled Lapita ware, in sites extending from the Admiralty and Bismarck archipelagoes down through the Solomons and New Hebrides to New Caledonia.

Another fairly certain reconstruction of Pacific-Island prehistory concerns Micronesia. It has already been mentioned that both archaeology and linguistics support the occurrence of a migration, from the west, of Austronesian-speaking peoples into the Palau and Mariana islands no later than about 3,600 years ago, a migration that differed somewhat in cultural composition and probably in geographic source from those of their Austronesian-speaking "cousins" whose eastward routes lay further south (and whose descendants eventually moved much further south and east). Until a few years ago it was believed by the experts that the northern, Palau–Mariana, branch of Austronesian-speakers went no farther east than there (or perhaps somewhat farther, to Nauru and Yap), and that the other Caroline islands had been first settled by peoples whose ancestors had reached there, in the course of centuries, via the Solomons (or the New Hebrides) and the Gilbert and Marshall islands. Linguistic evidence still supports the occurrence of such movements, but more recent evidence from archaeology suggests that some descendants of the Palau–Mariana pioneers had moved much further east and had already occupied many of the Caroline islands that their westward-moving counterparts were supposed to have pioneered.

Such will continue to be the fate of most detailed schemes of reconstruction concerning Pacific Islanders' prehistory. But there is one general proposition about that prehistory that will certainly stand the test of time, and that is that the movements of peoples and ideas and artifacts among these far-flung islands will be found to be much more numerous and complex than is now known.

Sources

Bellwood 1979; Blust 1980; Dixon 1980; Flood 1983; Grace 1966; Howells 1973; Jennings 1979; Pawley 1972; Pawley and Green 1973; White and O'Connell 1982; Wurm 1975; Yen 1973, 1974, 1980.

CHAPTER THREE

Activities

INTRODUCTION

WHAT kinds of cultures had the Islanders constructed by the time Europeans first saw them?

Note well the plural, "kinds": there were hundreds of sharply distinguished cultures in place when Europeans first arrived upon the scene (which should not occasion surprise, in view of the many historical and geographical variables in the region, as summarized in chapters 1 and 2). The culture of every human society is distinctive in at least some respects, but the differences that prevailed among those of the Pacific Islands were so numerous and in many instances so wide that any attempt to classify them, in order to generalize about them, is fraught with difficulties.

The usual, the anthropologically standard, classification has been into three major divisions: Polynesia (from Greek *poly,* 'many' + *nesos,* 'island'), Micronesia (from Greek *mikros,* 'small'), and Melanesia (from Greek *melas,* 'black'). The first of these labels is the least arbitrary; the twenty or so societies of people who occupied the widely scattered islands of this division spoke closely related languages, shared many cosmological beliefs and religious practices, and ordered their social relationships in many similar ways, all as a result of their relatively recent derivation from a single cultural source. On the other hand, the no less relevant subsistence technologies of the Polynesians were widely diverse, ranging from total dependence upon fishing and one or two tree crops to cultivation of a wide variety of vegetables, fruits, and nuts.

Turning to the islands now known as Micronesia, we see that they are indeed small (as were also many of those of Polynesia and Melanesia), but four of the languages spoken in this division were only very distantly related to the many other, more closely interrelated ones. Moreover, although several societies of central Micronesia had similar cosmologies,

social institutions, and subsistence technologies, those of the western and southeastern ends of this division differed markedly in many cultural respects from those of the center and from each other. For Melanesia, the cultural diversity that prevailed among the hundreds of societies lumped together under this label was of a scale large enough to accommodate forty or fifty subdivisions comparable with Polynesia in terms of homogeneity.

In other words, the usual three-fold division of the Pacific Islands and their native cultures is even less discriminating than would result from dividing the United States into, say, Maine, the rest of New England, and all the other states. So, how best to proceed, to provide the non-anthropologist reader with an informative description of the numerous and diverse cultures of this huge region, one that is neither impracticably encyclopedic nor deceptively simplistic? Doubtless, no two anthropologists would proceed in exactly the same way, because of their individual differences in research experience and topical interest. The way *this* anthropologist will proceed (not necessarily the best way) will be in two steps. The first will consist of a catalog of some of the activities that were engaged in nearly everywhere (e.g., where people resided; how they obtained their food; how they traveled on water; how they fought and traded; and how they responded to the pan-human drive of sex and to the pan-human events of birth, maturation, and death). The second step will consist of a broad survey of how they related to one another, socially, in doing all the above. This two-step separation, into activities and social relations, is of course arbitrary, as is any descriptive procedure that treats with cultures piecemeal, but in the face of the region's cultural complexity (and of book-publishing realities!) it is the most practicable one I can devise.

Harking back to the first sentence of this chapter, it should be recorded that the "discovery" of Pacific Island peoples and cultures, by Europeans, took place over a period of centuries: from 1521, when the Spanish landed at Guam, to a few years ago, when some bands of New Guinea natives were contacted by Europeans for the first time. This means that the pristine native cultures summarized in the following chapters were not observed, and recorded, at the same time (i.e., at the same periods of their respective histories). The weight to be attributed to such discrepancies cannot be measured, but the reader should not forget them when reading the rest of this book. And speaking of pristine, no native culture remained so for long after any firsthand encounters with Europeans. (In many cases the very sight of European ships induced changes in native cosmologies, and the observed effects of European firearms undoubtedly influenced native politics.) In fact, by the times of the observations on which most of the following descriptions are based, most of the peoples written about had, for example, replaced their stone axes with metal ones and their nearly inveterate warfare with a measure of colonialist peace.

Throughout the rest of this book frequent use will be made of several key words, words that have so many shades of meaning in our everyday usage that they require more precise definition for their more technical employment here; at the outset the following will suffice:

social group: any kind of aggregate of persons who interact with one another, directly or seriatim, with some regularity (e.g., the more or less permanent members of a domestic dwelling, the regular members of a gardening team or fishing crew). Among the Pacific Islanders the most ubiquitous kinds of social groups were households and communities.

households (called "domestic groups" in many writings): consisted of persons who regularly slept in the same abode (a single room or building, or a separate complex of buildings) and who shared in the production and consumption of food. Island households varied widely in size, from one person (usually a widowed individual) to up to twenty or more. In most cases all or most of the members of any household were related by family ties. (The various types of families found in the Islands will be considered later on; for the present the common English usage of the word family will serve. The same informality applies to my use of the label clan, which for present purposes will be used to refer to any kind of unit of kinfolk wider than the family.) Throughout the Islands nearly all households were components of communities.

community: a distinct cluster of households. In most recorded cases the members of any Pacific Island community shared enough sentiments of unity, and of difference from other communities, to dispose them to interact among themselves in relatively peaceful and cooperative ways, and to settle disputes among themselves by means short of unbridled killing. In many places community members also joined together to work, to fight outsiders, to feast, and to engage in religious rites. Pacific Island communities ranged in size from about twenty persons to more than a thousand, and in spatial separateness from almost total isolation (as on some small islands and in some forest fastnesses) to virtual junction with like units (e.g., adjacent ones on some densely populated atolls).

society: a social unit composed of persons who resided adjacently and who shared, more or less distinctively, a common culture (i.e., a common set of premises, values, and practices, including usually a common language). In some parts of the Islands a single, usually isolated, community constituted a whole society as well, but in most cases a society contained two or more communities. Unlike single communities, some societies were riven, occasionally or chronically, by warfare. However, for the members of any one society the behavior of co-members would have been comprehensible, no matter how personally obnoxious it may have been. Throughout this book, "a people" will often be used to refer to all members of any one society, "peoples" to the members of more than one.

The ethnographic literature on the Pacific Islands contains many different usages of the word tribe. In some writings it refers to what I call a community, or to two or more communities that combine to do something together (most typically, to fight against a common enemy). In other reports the word tribe is used to refer to what I label a society, in still others to all peoples speaking the same language or dialect, or is used so imprecisely or inconsistently as to defy comprehension. Rather than compound this confusion, I will avoid using the troublesome word in the present book and rely on adjectives and verbs to indicate what particular communities of people do in common, including how they are governed (which will be discussed in chapter 4).

I begin this catalog of Islanders' activities with an account of where and how they were domiciled.

DOMICILE

The three and a quarter million or so Islanders of pre-European times were spread very unevenly over their islands' half-million square miles of land, as a consequence of several, largely interdependent, conditions, including especially the region's wide geographic diversity and the peoples' many different ways of obtaining food. Within each society's more or less exclusive territorial boundaries, the population densities ranged from two or three up to 2,600 per square mile, the former in some mountainous areas of New Guinea and New Zealand, the latter on an atoll islet in the central Carolines.

Geography and ways of food getting also influenced the size of a society's component communities, but other factors, such as kin relations and warfare, were influential as well.

The spatial layouts of Island communities may be classified, and not too arbitrarily, into two major types: nucleated and dispersed. The former were exemplified in compact villages, where the boundaries of households directly adjoined each other, or, in some cases (mostly in New Guinea), where each family–household occupied a room in a communal "long house." In contrast, the dispersed type of community layout was exemplified in places where each household's buildings were located, either singly or in small hamlet clusters, at intervals of up to hundreds of yards.

As for the architecture of Islanders' household buildings, their shapes and sizes were too diverse to attempt to classify and describe in words; instead, the accompanying drawings (Fig. 3.1) will provide an impression of some of them.

Figure 3.1. House types: *a*, New Guinea, Gulf of Papua, Orokolo; *b*, New Caledonia; *c*, Palau; *d*, Tahiti; *e*, Hawaii; *f*, New Zealand

d

e

f

In some societies a household's distinctive use-areas (e.g., for sleeping, cooking, eating, receiving guests) were housed in separate buildings and yards; in others all or most of these different use-areas were located in the same house, but not, usually, in separate rooms (i.e., in very few places were houses divided into partitioned rooms). Two examples, chosen at random, will illustrate the nature of some such arrangements (scores of examples would be required to illustrate their wide diversities).

The first is that of the Tikopia, a society of some 1,280 Polynesian-speakers who inhabited a small isolated island at the extreme southeast of the Solomons chain. (In fact, most of their descendants still live there, and in ways not altogether unlike those of their forefathers referred to here. Nevertheless, in this chapter and in chapter 4, all statements about Island peoples and cultures will be phrased in the past tense, whether or not they still prevail.)

A typical Tikopian household occupied an enclosed ground-level main house, an adjoining cooking shed, and a canoe shed on the beach nearby. The rectangular unpartitioned floor-space of the main house was divided, "socially," into three parts: a side part reserved for cooking, where women and children usually sat; the opposite-side part (toward which no one was supposed to turn his back), which contained the graves of former family members, and which was used only during religious rites and then only by men; and the broad central part of the house in between, where any member of the house could sit, eat, sleep, etc. Aside from cooking ovens hollowed out in the ground, the principal "furniture" of the house was the four posts supporting its roof; each of these served as a backrest for the household's senior male members or for distinguished male guests. The small, crawl-in doors of the house were also allocated: an end one for the senior male householder, the opposite end one for men to use on ceremonious occasions, and side ones for women and children and for men's everyday uses. And finally, each house was oriented so that its "profane" (i.e., kitchen) side was inland, facing the gardens and groves, and its "sacred" side seaward, facing the beach and the canoe shed (which was exclusive to males).

A second example of household spatial arrangements is that of the Caroline island of Yap, whose pre-European population of 20,000 or so was divided into some 150–200 class-stratified communities. Each household on Yap had its own sleeping house and one or more cook-houses. The former was usually built on part of a large stone platform, whose outside surface, the porch, served as a general sitting area for occupants and guests. Inside, the sleeping house was divided by a log into two sections. The back section was reserved for the (male) household head; in it was his sleeping place, his own valuable possessions, and the household's sacred objects (which were used by him, as household priest, in prayers to ancestors). The household's adult women and young children slept in the front section of the house, its older unmarried girls in the cookhouse. A community's older unmarried boys all slept together in a separate house of their own.

In addition to their household buildings, the communities of most Pacific Island societies contained buildings or cleared areas of one or another of the following types: meeting houses for all community residents, or for all older males; work sheds (especially, in coastal communities, for building and storing boats); temples and burial grounds; archery ranges; dance grounds; and so forth. And in many societies, the whole territory of each of their communities was divided into areas where some persons (e.g., menstruating women, females in general, outsiders) could not go.

In summary, although the nucleation or dispersal of a community's household buildings was not necessarily correlative with its degree of social unity, the nature of its public buildings and areas provides useful clues about many of its institutions. An example from the Solomon Islands will serve to illustrate.

The 2,200 or so Baegu-speakers occupied a 61-square-mile mountainous area of northern Malaita. Baegu territory was divided into *lolofaa* (communities) and these into *fera* (hamlets). (Some large *lolofaa* were further divided into two or more distinct subcommunities of *fera*.) Each *lolofaa* was identified with one or another of the Baegu's clans and contained within its territorial boundaries that clan's ancestral shrine; it was, thus, a religious as well as a kin-based residential unit. Each *fera* consisted of two or more nuclear-family households (i.e., one consisting of a husband, his wife or wives, and their offspring), and each household had its own house, called a *luma,* used by all family members. Also, the men and youths of a *fera* had houses *(bisi)* of their own, where they spent much of their time and which were off limits to females. In addition, the senior man of a *fera* had a house of his own, also denied to females, where he represented the *fera*'s residents in petitions to the spirits of their recently deceased kinfolk. Women as well had houses of their own, in isolated and hidden places: one for giving birth and one for residence during menstruation. Both of these places were avoided by males, mainly because of beliefs about the pollutive condition of women during menstruation and childbirth. In fact, a male Baegu's fear of the pollutive influence of women carried over into the topographic layouts of both *luma* and *fera*. Thus, when a household's youths and men slept in their separate houses, its females customarily slept at the downhill, back end of the *luma.* And in laying out a *fera* the part of it associated with men was always located uphill (because, it was believed, women's "pollution" flowed downhill).

All Island households and communities were laid out according to plan, although not, of course, according to the same kind of plan. And although terrain was a factor in most such plans, other considerations, such as kinship, gender, age, rank, and religion, also entered into their formulation, although with many different emphases and permutations.

BOATS AND OCEAN TRAVEL

Without boats there would have been no people in the Pacific Islands. At no time during the span of *human* presence in Southeast Asia has the ocean gap between that region and the nearest Pacific island (i.e., New Guinea) been less than about 36 (nautical) miles, and it is unlikely that enough humans could have swum that gap, even with the support of logs, to establish a reproductively viable colony on the eastern side. On the other hand, rafts or small bark or dug-out canoes would have enabled people to cross that gap, and in fact to have borne pioneers even beyond New Guinea's eastern shores, as far east as Rossel, New Britain, and New Ireland. Beyond those and their offshore islets, however, the nearest habitable islands are Buka and Bougainville, over 100 miles farther east, and watercraft capable of crossing those gaps would have had to be more seaworthy than the prototypes just mentioned. Once developed, however, such craft could, and evidently did, carry people as far south and east as San Cristobal and, with a few more improvements, to New Caledonia (which was and remained the end of *that* voyaging line).

The next stage in man's movement into the Pacific occurred in two different places. The earlier, at least 3,600 years ago, was from Indonesia or the Philippines (or possibly from northwestern New Guinea) to the western Carolines and the Marianas. The second, about 3,000 years ago, was from the New Hebrides to Fiji. The shortest ocean gaps involved in both of these movements, about 500 miles, could have been crossed by enough people (enough to establish reproductively viable populations) only in sail-propelled boats that were fairly large and reasonably stable, which in these instances turned out to be canoes with outriggers or double hulls. With such boats as these, the descendants of those pioneers were able to reach and settle all but three of the Islanders' farthest outposts: namely, Easter Island, New Zealand, and Hawaii, which were separated from their nearest way stations by distances, respectively, of 1,300, 1,700, and 1,890 miles. Those voyages, which took place between about A.D. 500 and 1000, required boats of a size, seaworthiness, and steerability comparable with those seen by Europeans a few centuries later. (The Vikings, whose much-heralded seafaring took place between A.D. 850 and 1350, achieved nonstop open-sea voyages no longer than about 500 miles.)

With such beginnings, it might be concluded that boats were an inherent part of Islanders' lives, and so they were for many of them. But to the many others who lived in inland areas without lakes and broad streams, boats had over time become forgotten, and even some coastal and riverine Islanders who knew of their existence did not own or use them, because, for example, of unmanageable seas and currents or of traditional adherence to land-bound ways.

Turning now to the types of watercraft in use by Islanders when Europeans arrived on the scene, we can begin with simple, wooden swimming supports. These were to be found in many places, from New Guinea to Easter Island, but it was in Tahiti and Hawaii that board riding became most highly developed and counted also as a sport. In Hawaii, surf playing on huge boards was engaged in by all classes of people, although aristocrats are said to have excelled in it (from frequent practice) and to have reserved the best surfing areas for themselves.

Rafts were also in use (usually in protected waters) in many places, from New Guinea to Mangareva. Their floating elements consisted either of wooden logs, bamboo poles, or bundles of reeds. In some cases the elements were lashed directly together, in others connected by cross strips of wood. In most places they were small and impromptu affairs; in some other places they were large and sturdily built, such as the sail-propelled *lakatoi*, which served to transport several persons and heavy cargoes for hundreds of miles along the shores of the Gulf of Papua.

By far the most common boats in the islands were canoes, of many sizes and shapes (Fig. 3.2). All of them had wooden hulls, but they differed from place to place in several other ways. First, with respect to their hulls: some consisted of nothing more than a single dug-out log; others of two or more dug-out sections joined together lengthwise; still others of a single or composite dug-out base deepened by the addition of wooden strakes; and still others of an almost flat keel deepened entirely with strakes. Second, some canoes were stabilized only by means of their broad beams or by the skilled balancing of their occupants; others by addition of an outrigger (or in a very few places, by two); and still others by the joining of two hulls. A third kind of variable in Island canoe structure was canoe size, which ranged from small one-person craft to sizes over 100 feet long and capable of carrying 500–600 persons. (For comparison, the largest of the Viking ships carried no more than about 200.)

In addition to those basic diversities, Island canoes differed, from place to place, in numerous other respects: in the manner of connecting outrigger floats to hulls, in height and shape of bows, in height of freeboards, and so forth. And although the basic principles of making and using canoes doubtless originated in Southeast Asia and beyond, every canoe-using society in the Pacific Islands seems to have developed special design features adapted to local conditions of water, weather, and use.

Propulsion of Island canoes (and of rafts) was by poling, sculling, paddling, and sail. Paddling was the most common method over short dis-

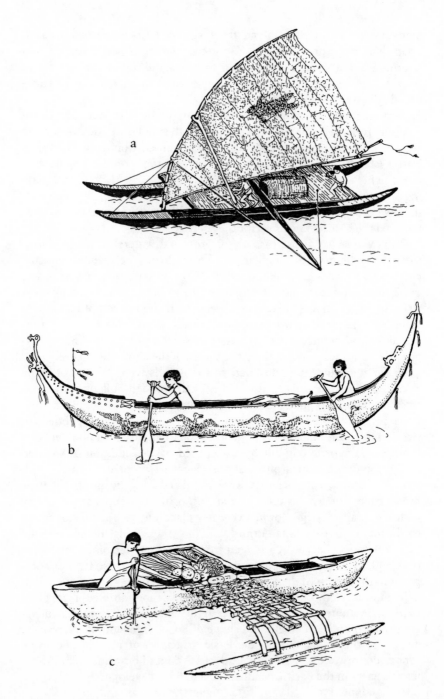

Figure 3.2. Boat types: *a,* Tonga; *b,* San Cristobal; *c,* Mokil, Caroline Islands; *d,* Tahiti; *e,* Gulf of Papua

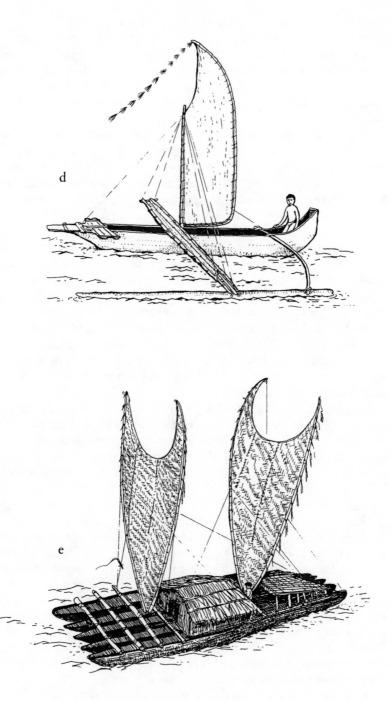

d

e

tances, but deliberate long voyages would have required sail. Recent tests indicate that experienced paddlers can maintain a three-knot pace for days on end—in calm water, that is, and with enough food and water to sustain their strength. The same tests showed that a slight current and a 20-knot headwind slowed the canoe to one knot, demonstrating that long, non-drift voyages would have been impossible without the help of sail.

When Europeans first arrived in the Islands, sails for the canoes were lacking throughout most of the Solomons and along some stretches of the New Guinea coast, and at the same time some other New Guinea peoples had only crude and makeshift rectangular sails. Elsewhere in the Islands, however, the sails, although widely diverse in other respects, were all more or less triangular, and seem to have derived from the ancient Indonesian boomed lateen sail.

In terms of performance under sail, single-outrigger canoes are superior to double-hulled ones, and among the former some of the most efficient of Island canoes were those of the central Carolines. When running before the wind, the latter have been found to be better in some respects than a modern racing catamaran of similar size, but cannot match the performance of a deep-hulled modern fore-and-aft-rigged boat when sailing into the wind. Comparisons aside, the large double-hulled canoes of Polynesia did in fact transport enough people and cargo over open-sea distances of up to nearly 1,900 miles to establish viable colonies in previously uninhabited places.

Needless to say, the building and operation of, especially, deep-sea canoes required much human knowledge and skill, but in the view of the Islanders success in these enterprises required supernatural help as well. Hence, the making and using of canoes were accompanied by many religious actions, including blessing of the makers' tools and supplication of spirits of wind and of sea.

Islanders used their boats for many purposes, including fishing, going to their gardens, visiting nearby places to trade or wage war, and so forth. In addition, many of them had through time used them for deliberate, long open-sea voyages to destinations either known or unknown. Reasons for such voyaging included trade, conquest, escape from enemies or from starvation at home, and even in some instances a desire for adventure. Numerous other long voyages had doubtless taken place involuntarily (i.e., by boats allowed to drift after being lost at sea). (In fact, some writers have asserted that even the most isolated Pacific Islands were colonized in this way, an opinion that has been challenged by recent studies of patterns of currents and winds.) But it is the deliberate voyaging to known destinations that concerns us now. And because there can be no doubt about the adequate steerability and carrying capacity of some types of Island canoes, the question becomes: did any Islanders possess enough knowledge to navigate successfully over long distances of open sea?

This question has provoked a great deal of scholarly (and unscholarly!) debate for a century and more, ranging from romantic and preposterous pros to flat and closed-minded cons. The difficulty came about because long open-sea voyaging had ceased in most places by the time Europeans had developed interest in it. But not everywhere. Until recently, a handful of Island men in a few places still retained the traditional knowledge and skills needed for long-voyage navigation, and a few of them have revealed their knowledge to visiting scholars (some of whom were experienced seamen themselves). According to the latter, their Island informants divided the approach to a known but distant destination into three stages. The first consisted of heading the boat in the known direction of the destination by lining up landmarks at the place of departure (e.g., mountain peaks, capes, tall trees); the second of maintaining the desired direction through the open seaway to the third stage of the voyage; that is, within "finding" distance of the destination (e.g., within sight of islands known to adjoin it; or by signs such as land-shaped ocean swells, land-based fishing birds, cloud colors reflecting vegetation or lagoons; and so forth). On long open-sea voyages it was the second stage that presented the greatest difficulties and encouraged the most ingenious solutions. During this stage, which could have lasted up to 3 or 4 weeks, the most commonly utilized direction markers were wind (and wind-generated wave), sea swells of known shape, currents of known speed, plus sun and, especially, stars. In this book it is not possible to catalog the numerous ways in which these markers were utilized by Island navigators. Suffice it to say that the knowledge they evinced, of meteorology, ocean topography, astronomy, etc., must be judged as being among the highest intellectual achievements of Pacific Islanders, knowledge that in some societies could only be acquired through lengthy study in navigation "schools" and through years of apprenticeship to navigation masters.

FOOD

Pacific Islanders obtained their food in one or more of the following ways: by growing plants; by collecting wild plants; by raising animals; by hunting and collecting wild animals, terrestrial or marine; and by trade with other Islanders. The focus on one or another of those sources varied widely. In some societies gardening supplied nearly all of the food eaten, with only minute amounts from other sources. In others the food supply came largely from semiwild plants, supplemented by daily servings of fish. And in still others (where, for example, fertile land was scarce) some locally caught fish was regularly traded for vegetables grown elsewhere. However, no matter how dependent any Islanders were on other sources of food, all of them were acquainted with the principle of plant cultivation (in which respect they differed fundamentally from the natives of nearby Australia).

Horticulture

The major cultivated food plants were coconuts, sago, breadfruit, pandanus, bananas, and numerous rootlike vegetables (Fig. 3.3). Rice, the sole cereal, was grown only in the Marianas.

The coconut palm *(Cocos nucifera)* needs year-round temperatures no lower than about 70° F; hence, it did not grow in New Zealand nor in any of the tropical islands at altitudes over about 1,000 feet. Where it did grow, it provided either a welcome supplement to the local starchy staples or, on a few coral islands, the principal plant food. Some coconut palms were doubtless self-propagated, but most of them were deliberately planted. A palm begins to produce nuts about 5 years after planting and continues to yield for another 40–60 years. The immature nut is filled with a tangy liquid that in time changes into a layer of hard white "meat" on the inner surface of the shell and finally into a spongy embryo. Islanders drank the liquid and ate the meat and embryo raw; in addition they shredded the meat and either cooked it in combination with other vegetables or expressed its cream and used it to oil other foods. In some places, principally in Micronesia, people collected the sap, or "toddy," from the coconut's blossoms and drank it, either fresh or fermented, or boiled it into a kind of candy.

The sago palm (*Metroxylon* spp.), 30–40 feet tall, grows in swampy soils throughout the islands north of New Caledonia and west of the Marshall and Cook islands. Though self-regenerative, it was in many places also deliberately planted. An almost pure starch was obtained from the pith of the palm's trunk by pulverizing and washing it; it could be stored for months without spoiling and was either baked, made into a porridge, or mixed and cooked with other foods. On the average, one palm yields 250–350 pounds of starch. In addition, the felled and harvested trunks become feasting grounds for grubs, which were a favorite food for many Islanders.

Breadfruit *(Artocarpus altilis),* which was deliberately grown mainly in the eastern and northern Islands, was also starchy but more variedly nutritious than sago. The core of its roundish fruit was cooked (usually baked) either fresh from the tree or after long fermentation; the latter was an accommodation to its seasonal ripening.

Many species of *Pandanus* thrived in the Islands, some cultivated, some wild. The pulpy, fatty phalanges of the fruit served mainly as a supplement to other staples in many places (e.g., in some mountainous parts of New Guinea), but one species, *P. tectorius,* which thrives in the thin soils of many central and eastern atoll islets, was some peoples' only vegetable food. The pithy parts of its phalanges were eaten either raw or cooked. Flour made from the fruit remained edible for months and helped to sustain life during long sea voyages and through periods of scarcity ashore.

The bananas (*Musa* spp.) grown in the Islands were the nonsweet, cooking (i.e., plantain) type. They were the principal staple in only a few places; wherever else they were grown (or sometimes collected from the wild) they served as supplements, usually to breadfruit or to root vegetables, to which we now turn.

Throughout the Islands, wherever root crops (mainly aroids, yams, and sweet potatoes) could be grown they usually were, and in most cases as a people's principal food. Among the aroids, "true" taro *(Colocasia esculenta)* was most widely distributed. It grew best in well-watered soils; for many peoples, it was the favorite food, but was highly perishable. "Swamp" taro *(Cyrtosperma chamissonis)* remained edible in the ground for years but was coarser and less favored than "true" taro. A third aroid, *Alocasia macrorrhiza,* was hardier and required less moisture than "true" taro but contained so many oxalate crystals that they had to be washed out before eating; it served mainly as a standby food.

The two species of yams (genus *Dioscorea*) most widely cultivated were *alata* and *esculenta;* both of these required more labor than "true" taro but remained edible for months after harvest. Moreover, with careful tending *alata* ("great" yam) could grow to lengths of 10 feet or so and although such specimens were too coarse for eating they were often grown and exhibited as evidence of the growers' gardening skill.

Sweet potatoes *(Ipomoea batatas),* a South American plant, entered the Pacific Islands along three different routes (one of them directly from South America in pre-Columbian times), and in each case spread rapidly as a favored food. Hardier and more adaptable than taro and yams, they permitted Islanders to subsist in drier and cooler settings, such as New Zealand and the Highlands of New Guinea. (And although the sweet potato of the latter area had entered the region in post-European times, it had become completely "nativized" before Europeans "discovered" that area.)

Other starchy root crops grown in the Islands had more localized distributions: for example, arrowroot *(Tacca leontopetaloides),* ti *(Cordyline terminalis),* turmeric *(Curcuma domestica),* and kudzu *(Pueraria lobata).*

Unlike some other methods of agriculture, whereby seeds are scattered over uniformly prepared ground, Islanders used mainly cuttings, which were planted one by one. Also, except for some composting and some

Figure 3.3. Food plants: *a, Cocos nucifera; b, Musa* sp.; *c, Artocarpus altilis; d, Metroxylon* sp.; *e, Dioscorea esculenta; f,*

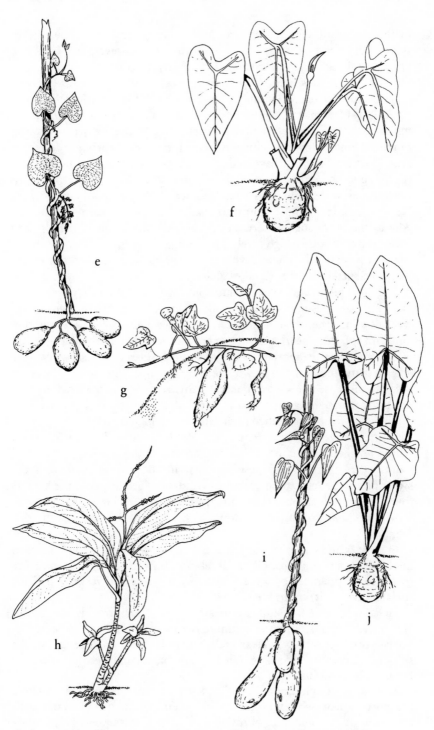

Colocasia esculenta; g, Ipomoea batatas; h, Cordyline terminalis; i, Dioscorea alata; j, Cyrtosperma chamissonis

deliberate use of ashes (from site-clearing fires), no fertilizer was used. Aside from these few area-wide uniformities, however, the Islanders' agricultural techniques varied widely, partly because of differences in physical conditions and crop peculiarities, but also because of less exigent cultural practices and ideas. In terms of what might be called agricultural "intensity" (the measure of technology that serves to econo- mize use of land), one extreme was represented by the many peoples who practiced long-fallowing, which involved little or no clearing or soil prep- aration or artificial drainage and replanting intervals lasting many years (i.e., due to soil exhaustion, real or imagined). The other extreme was represented, for example, by some peoples of New Caledonia and of the New Guinea Highlands, who were enabled to use the same site repeat- edly by measures such as terracing, drainage ditching, soil turning, and composting. Another high level of technology was exemplified by irriga- tion, the peak of which was developed by the Hawaiians, who, for exam- ple, constructed (on the island of Kauai) a stone and clay aqueduct ditch over 20 feet high. The consummate application of technology was, how- ever, located on some soil-less atolls of the central Pacific, where pits were dug into the coral fundament and filled with decaying vegetation and with soil from nearby islands to grow otherwise ungrowable crops.

Through one or another of the above measures most Islanders were able to grow most of their own vegetables. Those who could not do so (usually because of environmental constraints) obtained what they needed from neighboring peoples, by trade, or moved to other places, or, doubtless in many cases, died in the attempt to migrate.

All the above concerns the tropical Pacific Islands. In New Zealand, whose northernmost cape is 700 miles south of the tropics, of the food plants taken there by Polynesian settlers in about A.D. 1000, only the sweet potato proved to be successfully adaptable. However, the settlers found other indigenous foods there, including the rhizomes of a large fern *(Pteridium esculentum),* along with a plentiful avian and marine fauna.

In most Island societies, agriculture occupied so much of the time of so many persons that almost all social relationships served in some measure to shape its practice, or were shaped by it. Here, however, only four social aspects of it will be mentioned.

First, in nearly all Island societies the basic food-growing social unit was the household. In many communities men from neighboring house- holds worked together to clear and prepare land for gardening, but the subsequent planting, weeding, tending, and harvesting were usually done by single households.

Second, although land clearing and site preparation were everywhere the work of men, who did the other gardening jobs varied from one soci- ety to the next. Some kind of division of labor always prevailed, usually based on gender, but planting (for example) was not done solely by one sex or the other everywhere. Another labor practice found in many Island societies was for males to tend one kind of crop and females another. Thus, in New Caledonia females tended taro (known locally as a "wet" crop, because of its need for more moisture) and males the "dry" yam. (In this case the contrast between the phallic-shaped yam and the triangle-shaped taro was linked with this labor division, as was perhaps the greater "wetness" of females.)

The third social aspect of Island agriculture deserving mention has to do with the ownership of food-producing land. With very few exceptions this and all other categories of land in Island societies were owned, corporately, by one or another kind of kinship unit, and usually by units larger than individual families or multi-family households. Household members joined together in working tracts of land and while doing so possessed use-rights (i.e., provisional title) to such tracts, but residual title to them usually remained with some larger kinship unit, most typically with a clan to which some or all of the household members belonged.

A fourth social aspect deserving mention is the value that many peoples attached to agricultural expertise, best exemplified in societies where gardeners competed in the size of their yams, or where produce was stored and publicly exhibited in elegant storehouses. Such expertise was seldom a sufficient basis for community leadership, but in most societies it did win community-wide esteem.

In many places there were also esthetic values attached to agriculture (e.g., care taken to build handsome fences or to standardize and align plots), but it is the religious side of the activity that merits further comment in this condensed survey.

To begin with, the mythical origins of its staple food crops figured prominently in nearly every people's cosmogony. Moreover, in nearly every society's pantheon some specific spirit or spirits (and typically some of the most powerful ones) were associated with each of their staples and, therefore, the recipient of supplications and thank-offerings. Also, in the magic pharmacopoeia of many peoples there were spells and materials that acted automatically to promote the growth of one's own crops, or to destroy those of one's enemies or rivals. All this does not mean that Islanders depended primarily upon religious acts to make their crops grow; nevertheless, except in a very few places such acts, however small and inconspicuous, were believed to be at least useful, and in some they were large-scale and public and considered to be indispensable.

Domestic Animals

When Europeans first saw them, most Island peoples kept and used for food one, two, or all three of the following: chickens, dogs, and pigs. The degree of domestication of those animals ranged from occasional feeding (enough only to keep them from permanently straying) to permanent penning, total nurturance, and controlled breeding.

Of the three, chickens were in most places the least tended and the least valued for food (their eggs were eaten rarely if at all). In only one society were they prominent; that was Easter Island, where they were fed well and used as valuable items of exchange, an importance probably due to their being the only domesticated animals to have survived the settlers' journey to that easternmost outpost.

Dogs were less ubiquitous than chickens and their uses more varied. In some societies they were only scavengers; in others they were semi-fed and used in hunting. But in a few (mainly in Polynesia) they were fattened, treated as pets, and eaten as delicacies.

Pigs were another matter altogether. As one New Guinean proclaimed, "Pigs are our hearts." Those thin-bodied, long-snouted exemplars of *Sus scrofa* were introduced into New Guinea by migrants from the west thousands of years ago, and after that accompanied Islanders in most of their migrations to the south and east of there—except to New Zealand and Easter Island, where they either were not taken or did not long survive. Nor were they found in any Micronesian islands when Europeans first landed in them. Their degree of domestication ranged from total feeding and permanent penning, to part-time feeding and free running, or to no feeding at all (which usually led to their going wild and being hunted). Most domesticated pigs ended up as food, typically the most favored food, but before suffering that fate they served as highly prized repositories of wealth and as intrinsically valued media of exchange (in connection, for example, with marriages, political rivalries, and religious offerings). Because of their own large requirements of (cultivated) food, domesticated pigs were nowhere numerous enough to be an ingredient of daily cuisine, and hence were eaten only on festive occasions. Nevertheless, they were in many societies such integral members of their owners' households that they were treated as pets, fed premasticated food (even in some cases breast-fed), and nurtured with magical rites like some of those used for humans.

Some writers assert that pig-raising in the Islands was uneconomical: that the effort usually expended on them cost more than the food value received. That in most cases was doubtless true, but it does not take into account the many other satisfactions that the animals provided to their owners.

Wild Plants and Animals

The first settlers in New Guinea, over 40,000 years ago, subsisted entirely on wild plants and animals (including fish), and their descendants, and subsequent immigrants, continued to do so until agriculture and animal domestication commenced (at least 4,000–5,000 years ago). With that long background, it is not surprising that hunting (the quest for larger land animals) and gathering (the collection of wild plants and of smaller land animals, including insects) persisted throughout the Islands even after the alimentary need for them was reduced. In some places the quarry was prized for the variety it added to the diet, in others for the materials it provided for other purposes, such as bone for tools, feathers for ornaments, and skins for drum heads. Moreover, the men of many Island societies valued hunting because of the sheer pleasure of the chase. With that said, however, it should be added that the effort expended in hunting varied greatly from society to society. Much of that variation was, of course, due to the local availability of game, in which connection, it will be recalled, the variety and number of land-based animals tended to diminish from west to east. Strictly cultural factors were also influential. Thus, in New Guinea, where wild animals in variety and in plenty were to be found nearly everywhere, a people's interest in hunting ranged from near indifference (as, for example, among some Highlands people) to focal attentiveness (as, for example, among some people in the Sepik area, where hunting wild pigs was a major activity of men and where the highly patterned distributing of a kill was the most important means of maintaining a community's social integration and spiritual well-being).

Turning to Polynesia, it is not surprising that the abundance of land-based animals in New Zealand, including some ostrich-sized flightless birds, encouraged the settlers to develop hunting into one of their central activities. Another Polynesian example is offered by the quest for wild-bird eggs. In perhaps most Island societies they were not sought after at all, and even when found were ignored. Not so on Easter Island, where the annual search for the eggs of the sooty tern became the society's most important ceremonial event, a contest whose outcome shaped the society's political structure for the ensuing year. In several other Polynesian societies the principal goal of hunting was for feathers, especially for (religiously symbolic) red and yellow ones. Thus, in Hawaii red-feather cloaks were emblematic of high rank (one such contained the plumage of some 80,000 birds).

Like hunting, the amount of food gathering engaged in by Islanders varied from society to society, and not only in consequence of the natural supply of edible wild life. In some parts of Melanesia, for example, the natives depended upon wild sago for most of their plant food; in other places, also having large stands of sago palms nearby, their starch was obtained only occasionally and used mainly when the preferred root crops were in short supply. *Pandanus tectorius,* which grew wild along the shores of many islands, is another example of this kind. In some places it was the favored food and its supply augmented by cultivation; in other places where it grew it was not eaten at all, even in times of food shortage.

Notwithstanding all such quantitative differences in hunting and gathering, in every Island society known about in this respect their members as a whole recognized, and gave names to, virtually every kind of nonmicroscopic wild animal and plant in their territory; and not only those they considered useful (for food, ornament, medicine, magic, etc.) but useless ones as well. Moreover, they not only identified them with distinctive names, but went on to classify them as well. Not surprisingly, such taxonomic systems varied from one society to another; and although none of them resembled closely the one devised by Linnaeus, each of those so far studied reveals a comparably logical elaboration of its people's cognitive premises (which were in turn often found to have been influenced by their daily activities).

Fishing

As with dry-land fauna, the number of species of freshwater fauna decreases in the Islands from west to east, and relative to an island's size and topography. The west-to-east diminution of saltwater fishes is less marked but nevertheless occurs: there are about 2,000 species in the waters around New Guinea and only about 625 around Tahiti. This, however, does not mean that, say, New Guineans as a whole caught and ate more marine animals than did the residents of eastern Pacific Islands. In fact, for most of the latter fishing was a daily activity and fish a very large part of their diets, while in some inland parts of New Guinea the waters contain only crawfish, eels, and two or three species of fishes, which were not fished for at all.

In those communities where fishing did take place, two or more of the following kinds of techniques were employed. Hands alone were used to catch molluscs and other slow-moving prey, and in some places fast-swimming fish as well, with or without prior poisoning of the water (with stupifying agents such as derris). Nets ranged in type from one-person dip- or throw-nets to long drag and sweep ones, or half-mile-long seines operated from canoes. Spears were propelled either by hand or by bow, and either while swimming or from shore or water shallows or canoes. Nooses were used in some places to catch a variety of prey, including eels and sharks. Traps varied in shape and size from small basketlike types to huge stone weirs. Angling, with or without bait, employed both hooks and gorges and was done from shore or shallows, or from stationary or moving boats. A widespread but less common method of obtaining fish consisted of impounding them in ponds; this technology attained the stage of large-scale fish farming in Hawaii. In addition to all such nondistinctive, universal techniques of fishing, some

Islanders used certain distinctive ones, including trailing a hook by the tail of a kite, or catching an octopus by using oneself as bait.

Considered all together, the tools and techniques employed by Islanders in fishing were more varied than their agricultural ones, not surprising in view of the much wider variety in the nature and setting of the harvest and of fishing's immensely deeper antiquity. With all that variety, however, the kind of labor employed in Island fishing was divided in much the same way: males everywhere performed the more vigorous, strength-demanding jobs, such as deep-sea fishing and underwater spearing, and women engaged in collecting fixed or slow-moving marine animals in shallow waters near shore. And, as in the case of their hunting and collecting on land, the Islanders' stores of knowledge of the waters in which they fished extended well beyond that required for traveling and for obtaining food.

Perhaps because of their more than usual chanciness, some methods of fishing employed by Islanders were accompanied by correspondingly large amounts of religious acts, including supplication of spirits, magical reinforcement of boats and equipment, and spirit-sanctioned measures for conserving marine life. And in many places fishing served to link otherwise hostile communities in peaceful coexistence (i.e., by engendering barter between coastal fishermen and inland gardeners).

Eating and Drinking

The daily diets of Islanders consisted almost everywhere of the same kinds of basic components: a large amount of one or two kinds of starchy vegetable, a smaller portion of some leafy vegetable, a small portion of animal flesh (if available), and (likewise, if available) salt or some condiment (e.g. ginger root, turmeric, scented leaves, nuts, crushed insects). Also nearly everywhere was the practice of preparing and eating only one large daily meal, usually in late afternoon, after the major work of the day was done. In addition, most Islanders ate a small breakfast of cold leftovers, plus tidbits picked up in between meals.

Most cooking was by broiling, by boiling (where there were clay pots, which was not everywhere), and by baking (which was done in earth-pit ovens containing heated stones).

Along with those region-wide similarities, however, there were some wide local differences: for example, in the amounts of animal flesh eaten (i.e., much more in the case of coastal and riverine peoples) and in elaboration of cooking (ranging from throwing a chunk of sago or taro onto hot ashes, to oven-baking a pudding made, say, of a starch base, coconut cream, and nuts). And although the day's main meal was almost always prepared at home (i.e., within the spatial and social confines of one's own household), there were wide differences in who did the cooking: in some societies only females, in others only males, in still others males and females, with, say, females doing the boiling and males the baking, or vice versa. In some places (e.g., the New Guinea Highlands), the men and older boys ate their household-prepared meals in their separate male-only houses; in most other places all householders usually ate their main meals at home, but not necessarily at the same "table"; there were many societies in which older males ate separately from all females, in some cases even separately prepared meals.

The commensal nature of households was emphasized in many societies by the practice of including a group's tutelar spirits in its meal, usually with offerings of token amounts of food.

Returning to the human members of Island households, although they shared in the production and consumption of a common food supply, it was unusual for all members to be permitted to eat the same things. Thus, in many societies females were prohibited from eating certain foods permitted to males; the reverse also occurred, though less commonly. Or, in some societies certain foods were denied to individuals on the bases of their younger age or of their unmarried state. Pregnancy, illness, and bereavement were perhaps in most societies accompanied by eating restrictions, and in many of them any individual engaged in one or another kind of special activity (such as deep-sea fishing, canoe-building, warfare, or religious rites) was required to abstain from eating certain foods. Most of the above food restrictions derived from, or were rationalized by, religious suppositions (e.g., pork was too "strong" [too dangerous, magically] for weaker persons, such as children and women), but in some societies the local food restrictions were avowedly based on social class, as, for example, in several Polynesian societies where the eating of delicacies like turtle flesh was reserved for persons of chiefly rank.

The most widespread type of eating restriction was that based on totemism, wherein whole aggregates of persons (most commonly, those interrelated by ties of common descent) were prohibited from eating some item believed to have a special spiritual relationship with themselves (most typically, with some species of animal believed to be linked with them through common ancestral ties).

Before turning to the beverages drunk by Islanders, at their daily meals or other times, a word needs to be added about feasting, which occurred on some occasion or another in every society (e.g., at births, marriages, and deaths; at times of crop harvests or large catches of fish; upon completion of public buildings or successful wars; at times of stately visits by important neighbors or by spirits; etc., etc.). By the definition herein followed, feasts were specially scheduled (i.e., not impromptu) meals shared by persons from two or more households, usually many more. Very commonly, but not invariably, the foods served at feasts included items locally regarded as delicacies and not ordinarily served at daily meals (e.g., pork, laboriously prepared puddings). In addition, feasts usually served purposes that were explicitly religious, or political, or both.

Now to beverages. In a few Island societies seawater was drunk during meals but in most of them plain water was the main, or only, mealtime drink. As mentioned earlier, the tangy liquid of an immature coconut was a favorite drink wherever the palms grew but usually only between meals (as was the case with coconut toddy in the few places where it was extracted). It should, however, be noted that fresh water was not easy to obtain everywhere; in many places people had to walk or canoe long distances for their daily supply. And in some of the higher coral "pancake" islands they had to crawl down narrow tunnels to small underground pools for it, or, during droughts, extract it from fish—or emigrate, or die.

The only other beverage drunk by Islanders (and that not everywhere) was a narcotic infusion of the pulverized root of a pepper-family plant, *Piper methysticum;* native names for it differed from language to language but it has come to be known generally as *kava.* In some places kava grew wild; in others it was cultivated. The drug produces soporific and euphoric moods, its potency diminishing with the dryness of the root. In some places (e.g., western Polynesia) it was drunk ceremonially; in others (e.g., eastern Polynesia and parts of Melanesia) individually and without ceremony, and in some places addictively and to a morbid degree.

Other drug or druglike substances used in some Island societies included hallucinogenic mushrooms, tobacco, and betel.

Use of the first has been reported from only one place, a society in the New Guinea Highlands, but they may have been used elsewhere as well.

Although tobacco was being grown and smoked by many New Guineans when Europeans first discovered them, the plant is American in origin and had spread into New Guinea from Portuguese settlements in the Moluccas.

The custom of betel chewing spread into the western Pacific Islands from Southeast, and ultimately, southern Asia, many centuries ago. It consisted of the use of three items: the nut of the *Areca catechu* palm; the leaf, bean, or stem of the *Piper betle* vine; and slaked lime, made of either seashells, coral, or mountain lime. The mixture was chewed like plug tobacco and eventually expectorated. The nicotine-like properties of the nut, combined with other properties of the mixture, produce a general feeling of well-being, including a diminution of hunger and fatigue, without impairing consciousness. (Constant use not followed by mouth rinsing also tends to blacken the teeth, which seems not to have been regarded as undesirable.) Where betel chewing was practiced (i.e., in the western half of the region), it was done occasionally as a means of diminishing hunger and fatigue but more commonly as an act of sociability (including a sharing of ingredients).

We turn now to the question: did Pacific Islanders eat enough of the right kinds of food? From the viewpoint of most Islanders, it is probably safe to say that they would have preferred more pork, or more of whatever of their delicacies were relatively scarce, but that they considered their own kinds of food to be entirely "right," indeed, far superior to those of their neighbors (who ate, or did not eat, say, pandanus or reptiles, etc., and who were viewed as barely human because of that!).

But how do the indigenous diets of the Islanders of the pre-European era look from the viewpoint of the modern science of nutrition? This second form of the question is impossible to answer. Not only have the relevant scientists derived their recommended dietary norms mainly from studies of modern industrialized peoples, but even from those skewed samples their findings often disagree. In the face of that disagreement and in the absence of enough reliable studies of Island peoples (now no longer possible because of the nonindigenous foods in most Islanders' diets), the only general response that can be offered to the question is the finding that single individuals, perhaps, but no Island *peoples* encountered by Europeans in their pristine native state were known to be dying out as result of malnutrition. They may not have lived as long or as painlessly as most present-day Europeans, but whether that can be attributed to their diets is an open question.

Another question concerning Islanders' food habits is did they on occasion eat each other? Is there any reliable documentary evidence for a once-popular European practive of labeling this region "The Cannibal Isles"?

The answer to this query is undeniably affirmative, but in a narrowly qualified way. First, cannibalism was not practiced in all Island societies, perhaps not in a half, or quarter, or even a tenth of them. Most of the Europeans who reported the occurrence of the practive received their "evidence" from members of noncannibalistic societies slandering their enemies, about whom man eating and such other abhorrent practices as incest and rampant sorcery were commonly charged. And second, in most documented cases of South Seas cannibalism it was not a source of food. In some cases it was employed as punishment (i.e., eating a part of an enemy was a supreme gesture of retribution and contempt); in others it served as a magical means of absorbing some of the victim's desirable attributes, such as his strength, special skills, or spiritual essence. There were, however, a few cases in which man-eating was engaged in for the purpose of enjoying a highly valued kind of food. Instances of this were exiguous but fairly widespread, the most numerous of them having occurred in Fiji, where chiefly despots kept their ovens hot for the bodies of human "long-pigs."

SEX

There is no credible evidence that the members, as a whole, of any Island society differed genetically from those of any other with respect to the intensity, time span, and other details of their sexual drives. Yet, there is no domain of behavior encompassing wider differences, from society to society, in the cultural ways those drives were manifested. Some of those differences may have resulted, more or less directly, from environmental factors (such as endemic debilitating diseases or low-density population), but most were consequent upon cultural causes too indirect or remote in time to trace.

One aspect of those differences has to do with a people's consensual attitude toward sexual activity. At one extreme were societies such as Tahiti, most of whose sexually potent members copulated frequently, pleasurably, and almost openly, a penchant reflected in their everyday conversation, their public entertainments, and their myths. At the other extreme were the Mae Enga of the New Guinea Highlands. Among these diligent farmers and fierce fighters, sexual intercourse was generally considered to be debilitating and magically dangerous, especially for males, whose fear of the pollutive effects of menstrual blood approached paranoia. Reflecting that attitude (whether as cause or consequence is not now traceable), Mae Enga bachelors always, and the married men usually, slept together in male-only houses located at some distance from the household buildings where their wives and children or sisters slept. Another negative attitude toward sex was exemplified by the trade-oriented Manus people of Great Admiralty Island (north of New Guinea), but there the basis was not men's fear of menstrual pollution but a universal sense of shame, even disgust, toward most kinds of anal and genital excretion: fecal, urinal, menstrual, and sexual. Along with this society-wide prudery there were stern penalties, both social and supernatural, against adultery, and (according to their ethnographer, Margaret Mead) even conjugal intercourse was considered to be ". . . something bad, inherently shameful, something to be relegated to the darkness of the night" (1930a:126).

A random sampling of other Islanders' attitudes toward sex would place most peoples somewhat nearer the positive, Tahiti-like extreme.

Figure 3.4. Wooden carvings showing seated position for inter-course: *a,* New Zealand; *b,* Santa Anna, Solomon Islands

For example, in the case of those I know best (i.e., the Siuai of Bougain-ville), although strict segregation was preserved between sexually active males and females in most nondomestic activities, sex was generally regarded as pleasurable and was relatively free of religiously inspired fears. And although some social sanctions prevailed there against extra-marital fornication, they were not very severe and not very effective.

But however negative their attitudes may have been toward sex, some members of every Island society did, at least occasionally, engage in sex-ual intercourse! The question is how, where, whereby, and with whom, did they do so? (In terms of a people's continuity this question is surely just as relevant as, for example, what they ate.) First, how?

What mostly distinguished Islanders (i.e., from Europeans) in this domain of behavior was how few of them engaged, as the standard prac-tice, in what some of them have labeled the "missionary" position of intercourse: namely, the female underneath and facing the man lying on top. Much more common in many Island societies was for the couple to face one another in sitting positions (Fig. 3.4); or, in others, for the male to kneel between the female's outstretched legs; or in still others, for them to lie facing together side by side; and in many, many societies, to lie side by side with the female's back against the man's front when wishing to escape notice by nearby sleepers.

Similarly, Island peoples differed widely with respect to the amount and standardized kind of coital foreplay, from none at all to lengthy and elaborate rituals involving every erogenous area.

No less did Island cultures differ in their rules about when an individual's sex life should begin. In some places boys or both boys and girls were allowed, even encouraged, to begin at least to play at coitus during childhood; in others girls were shielded from it until well after puberty; in still others (such as some in the New Guinea Highlands) males commenced sexual activity, and that fearfully, long after the appearance of signs of puberty. Just as widely different were conventions regarding the termination of sexual activity. In some societies it was considered appropriate and seemly only among the relatively young; in others it was a matter of boastful pride to continue having sex as long as possible.

Island cultures also contained rules concerning when an individual's sexual activities should be curtailed. For example, in most societies of Melanesia and Micronesia women had to forgo copulation during their menstrual periods; in fact, in many of them they were required at such times to reside in separate and secluded huts, either alone or in company with other menstruating women. Also, conventions obtained in most Island societies about how long after parturition a woman should refrain from sex. In some places it was only a few days, until she healed; in many others it lasted until after the child was weaned, for periods of up to 3 or 4 years.

The restrictions just listed usually applied only to women; their husbands had to remain continent only if they were monogamous and were unable to engage in extramarital affairs. Restrictions on men's sexual activities were of other kinds (e.g., in some societies during their participation in religious activities or before going into battle or setting out on deep-sea fishing).

We turn now to the whereby of sexual intercourse (i.e., by what signs and other means Islanders sought to attract sexual partners). Unlike Europeans, males showed little or no sexual interest in women's breasts, which nearly everywhere were left uncovered. On the other hand the vagina was everywhere a powerful erotic sign; even in societies where women wore no garments they took pains to conceal it by holding their legs together when seated or lying down. In contrast, in only a few societies did males attempt, unequivocally, to conceal their genitals; in most places that concealment, by means of various kinds of G-strings or penis sheaths, seemed rather to emphasize than to hide.

Other signs deemed erotic by this or that Island people included head hair (in some places left bushy and long, in others cut short), face hair (in some places left to grow, in others plucked clean), and obesity (which was assiduously nurtured in some Polynesian societies). Tatoo (a Polynesian word); cicatrization; artificially molded heads; and pierced ear lobes, nasal septums, or nasal tips also served here or there as erotic signs, but such operations were usually performed for other purposes as well. And to all the above should be added the special garments, flowers, feathers, leaves, oils, and pigments that were worn in this or that society for erotic enhancement.

Actions also served Islanders as erotic signs: not hand-holding, however, which usually signified only friendship, between males and between females; and not lip-to-lip kissing, which came to be regarded as a disgusting European practice. Instead, Islanders expressed their desire for sexual relations by means of surreptitious gestures, stealthy messages, and in many societies (especially Polynesian) by dance movements that were explicitly, even flauntingly, copulatory.

It will come as no surprise to read that Islanders also used magical measures to attract sexual partners. Some of the overt practices already listed, such as body painting, were believed by some peoples to achieve their ends partly through magic, but reference here is to practices that relied wholly on supernatural means. Most of these were similar to the ones used in sorcery, except that the object was not to harm the victim but to seduce her (or him; females also utilized such means). In some societies such acts were carried out surreptitiously, having been considered a form of theft; in others they were engaged in openly and either by individuals or by groups of males or females.

Every Island society had rules concerning whom one could not marry, and most of them also had rules concerning whom one should marry. Generally speaking, the categories of persons forbidden to marry were also forbidden to engage in extramarital sex, although the penalties for violating the latter were usually not as severe. We can postpone discussion of whom one should marry and focus here on the prohibited categories of sexual, including marital, partnerships.

Every Island society prohibited sexual relations in general, and marriage in particular, between a female and her uterine sons and between a female and the man commonly believed to have sired her (in one way or another). In addition, except in Hawaii, where those of very high social rank were permitted, even encouraged, to marry, every society prohibited sex (including marriage) between uterine siblings. Moreover, the social sanctions, almost universally severe, that supported these several prohibitions were usually reinforced by supernatural ones as well, including spirit-induced sickness or death. Beyond this nuclear-family incest zone, however, societies differed widely with respect to which other categories of kinfolk, both consanguines and affines, should not marry or engage in sex. As will be described, kinship was the primary kind of social relationship in all Island societies, but there were many differences with respect to how kinfolk, as locally defined, were categorized (and ipso facto labeled) and how far kinship extended beyond the conjugal (the nuclear) family. Thus, in many societies an individual had several "mothers" (e.g., all of his own mother's sisters and all female same-generation members of her own clan). In such societies as these a male was usually forbidden sex (and of course marriage) with any of his "mothers," and penalties usually attended violation of the rule but with diminishing severity the more distant the kinship tie.

In several societies, mostly Polynesian ones, there were additional rules that discouraged sex and prohibited marriage between persons of different social class, as will be described in chapter 4.

Beyond these two factors of kinship and social class, there were few widely shared criteria concerning which persons should or should not engage in sex with one another. Peoples of many societies ridiculed, but none prohibited, marriage between persons of widely discrepant ages. In fact, it was the practice in many societies for older women to initiate callow youths, and older men young girls, into the locally favored copulation techniques. And although young persons were doubtless swayed by comeliness (as locally defined) in choice of lovers, industriousness was in most places more influential in choice of spouse—kinship, social class, and politics aside.

The norms about sexual relations just listed had to do with "everyday" sex. In addition, in many Island societies there were occasions on which many of those norms were officially suspended, when members of a community violated, without penalty, one or more of its customary sexual rules. Such violations ranged from general but furtive spouse swapping to unbridled public orgies. The kinds of events that, here or there, occasioned them included mass visits from other communities; accomplishment of some community enterprise, such as a fish-drive or battle; death of a chief; and religious ceremonies containing fertility themes.

Another institutionalized form of sexual license practiced in some Island societies was prostitution; not gift giving between lovers, which took place everywhere, but practices involving females as full-time purveyors of sexual services for subsistence or other recompense.

Finally, there were several Island societies in which one or another form of homosexual relations was legitimated, and even prescribed. These ranged from occasional homosexual acts between otherwise heterosexual friends, to "career" prostitution by homosexual males, or to institutions (mainly in Melanesia) in which all of a community's young men went through a years-long period of group-organized homosexual activity before "graduating" to the status of adult and marriage-ready men (such practices usually were believed necessary for promoting their maturation and growth).

REPRODUCTION

In perhaps all Island societies there were some individuals who for some personal reason or other wished to avoid having any, or any more, off-spring. In many of them whole categories of females were forbidden to bear offspring during certain periods of their lives (e.g., unmarried girls, nursing mothers). And in at least one society, Tahiti, the members of a cult, the Arioi, were encouraged to copulate but forbidden to procreate (i.e., any progeny produced by an active member was either aborted or killed at birth). Except for the above situations, however, the peoples of all Island societies considered the reproduction of new members to be an important and desirable activity, although ideas differed widely as to how it was accomplished.

In only two known Island societies, Trobriand and Yap, was it believed that coitus had nothing to do with procreation (i.e., that the fetus was a preexistent spirit, which entered the womb from outside to be nourished there until birth). In a few others coitus was viewed as serving only to open a path into the womb for the extraneous fetus-becoming spirit. But in most Island societies the fetus was believed to be a product (with some supernatural assistance) of the female's blood, or the male's semen, or both. (In a widespread variant of the latter the fetus' bone was believed to be produced by the semen, its flesh by undischarged menstrual blood.) Aside from the relevance of the above to a people's biological concepts, such beliefs also had a bearing on how they viewed the nature of, and the social relationships of, the resulting human being. Thus, an individual created only or mainly out of his mother's blood was ipso facto more closely related to the kin of his mother than to those of his, procreatively irrelevant, father, or so it could be logically inferred, and so in many societies it was explicitly considered to be.

Once a fetus was perceived to have been formed (say, by such signs as belly swelling or cessation of menstruation), most Island peoples had practices to promote its development (if it was wanted) or to end its existence (if not). The latter included use of magically acting abortifacients, or physical pummeling of the woman's abdomen, or, if these did not work, by infanticide. Conversely, measures to promote development of a wanted fetus included restrictions on the mother (e.g., prohibition of "dangerous" foods) and in some societies on the genitor as well (e.g., taboos against the killing of certain game).

Turning back a step, in many places methods were used to avoid unwanted pregnancies or to facilitate wanted ones that were slow to occur. The former included total sexual abstinence (e.g., while a woman was still nursing her latest infant, the so-called postpartum sex taboo), coitus interruptus, or use of magic-acting brews. The latter precaution, usually blamed upon the female, was countered by religious measures or, often, by acquisition of another wife.

Another phase of reproduction that Islanders institutionalized in widely different ways was parturition itself. In a few societies, especially Polynesian ones, the event occasioned few if any rites or restrictions: anyone, including males, could attend and assist in delivery; the mother resumed everyday activities, including sexual, as soon as she was physically able; no religious rites were performed; and so forth. At the other extreme were many societies, especially in Melanesia, where birth took place in special and secluded huts with no males present; where mother and child were "protected" by means of months-long seclusion that involved numerous magical measures and (ofttimes deleterious) dietary restrictions; and where the mother was required to forgo sex until the child was wholly weaned. If all Island societies were arrayed along an axis between those extremes, most of them would fall nearer the latter pole. That is to say, most of them imposed some cultural (arbitrary) restrictions on who could attend births and on the mother's subsequent activities.

Just as Island peoples differed in their treatment of biological birth, they also did so regarding social birth; that is, in their ideas and practices concerning when and how, after conception, a human organism became enough of a "person" to deserve the minimal rights, etc., extended to all other living members of its community. (Differences regarding this question also prevail between and within modern, "enlightened" nation-societies, as every newspaper reader knows.)

The range of such beliefs and practices was extremely wide. First, regarding the status of a fetus, I know of no Island society in which it was viewed as possessing fully, or even fractionally vested citizenship rights. In most of them its demise was totally ignored, except of course by its parents and except for efforts, in some places, to counteract and revenge any sorcery held responsible for the death. In some other societies whose members attributed a soul to it, that soul was thought to enter into, or actually become, another living being, either harmless (such as a periwinkle, because of its innocence) or malevolent (such as a shark, because of its anger), or into another fetus, for eventual rebirth.

Consistent with the above, in no Island society that I know of was a person vested with full citizenship rights immediately after birth. (In Tahiti the heir to an important kin-Title succeeded to that Title at birth, but only to the religious–ceremonial status associated with it.) Such rights, which everywhere differed according to sex and in many societies with social class as well, accrued only with the passage of time, and in most places with the performance of rites of some kind (religious, or social, or both). The religious components of such rites included acts to protect the still-vulnerable immature individual from malevolent spirits and to encourage his growth and future welfare; the social rites, to cement ties between the parents' respective relatives, and in some cases to legitimate the parents' marriage, and coincidentally their progeny's "citizenship."

Every Island society, like all other human societies, divided its members' passage from social birth to biological death into a number of stages, each of them labeled (e.g., infancy, childhood, youth, maturity, old age), and each of them defined by distinctive attributes (e.g., suckling during infancy; physical strength and stamina but lack of mature judgment during youth; physical decay, etc., during old age). Moreover, Island societies, like those elsewhere, signalized transition into some of those stages by special rites. In the absence of "birthdays" (I know of no Island people that marked an individual's age in solar years), timing for an individual's passage from one stage to the next was most commonly based on bodily signs (e.g., ability to walk, appearance of pubic hair, enlargement of breasts, or the onset of muscular flabbiness and physical decrepitude), although in some societies social events served to do so (such as nuptial rites, which in many places marked the change from youth to adulthood).

Readers, by now accustomed to expecting cultural differences among Island societies, will not be surprised to learn that they prevailed also with respect to an individual's passage through life; indeed, that they differed so widely that one might conclude that we had to do with different primate species. Thus, in some societies the full rights and responsibilities of adulthood (as locally defined) were attained during (physical) adolescence, in others only upon marriage or, even later, upon the bearing or siring of offspring. And although a stage of old age was conceptualized in every Island society and usually associated with progressive decrepitude, attitudes toward the aged varied from deep respect, even reverence, to contempt and heartless neglect. Especially diverse were practices concerning the universally human, indeed mammalian, process of physical and sexual maturation.

In some societies a male's transition from childhood to adulthood took place without formal recognition except perhaps for a label applied to the postchildhood but not-yet-adult phase, or except for some minor, private action regarding the individual boy, as in the case of the supercision (i.e., foreskin slitting) of boys in some Polynesian societies. At the other end of the range were the practices among many peoples of Melanesia of segregating and secluding boys in groups for months or even years and of subjecting them to prolonged terrorism (i.e., by imagined demons) and excruciating physical operations (e.g., hazing, foreskin removal, sodomizing, nostril piercing, forced vomiting) to the accompaniment of instruction in religious mysteries. In many such societies the boys who shared those experiences constituted a peer group, a closely knit "age set" that continued to function as a solidary unit for the rest of their lives.

In most Island societies a girl's first menstruation was announced publicly in some way; it was in many cases a sign of readiness for marriage, but in none that I know of was a girl's transition from childhood heralded with as much public attention, etc., as occurred in many places for boys. As a minimum, a menstruating girl was restricted in some activities (e.g., preparing food for males), and in many places all menstruating females, young and old, resided in secluded huts, alone or in company, during their periods. In addition, there were some societies in which a girl after her first menstruation was limited in what she could eat and do, and where she could go, for periods of weeks or months. But nowhere in the Islands did girls experience the degree of treatment, painful as well as privileged, that many societies meted out to boys of corresponding age.

The next culturally defined stage of life was adulthood, which in nearly every Island society encompassed marriage.

MARRIAGE

Sometime during his (or her) life nearly every Islander became "married." What being married was differed from one society to another, but everywhere included at least publicly approved sexual cohabitation, the sharing of labor and subsistence goods in a common household economy, and the co-parenting of the woman's progeny born during the marriage. The motives that led Islanders to marry differed somewhat from one society to another (and doubtless among members of the same society as well), but common to most Island peoples was their lack of socially defined roles for older bachelors and spinsters. (In other words, not to marry was almost unthinkable.) I will begin the résumé of this institution by listing how Island males obtained their wives. Instances occurred in which the reverse took place, but custom nearly always left initiative with the male side of the relationship.

Genuine forcible bride capture occurred in only a few places, mostly in Melanesia, and in those it was unusual (e.g., a windfall of victorious raiding). There were, however, a few other Island societies in which simulated bride capture was practiced, in some even as the most acceptable way of obtaining a wife.

A second, and very widespread, way of obtaining a wife was by inheritance: by acquiring, ofttimes automatically, the widow of one's brother or the sister of one's deceased wife. (The latter, labeled sororate marriage, was usually viewed as an action of replacement; the former, called the levirate, as a way of providing the widow with domestic security.)

Obtaining a wife by elopement may have occurred, as the rare exception, in all Island communities, but was socially acceptable for its own members in none. Unless the couple found safe haven in another community, they were required, eventually, to reconstitute their union according to the rules of marital contract in their own communities, to which we now turn.

In virtually all Island societies the most common route to marriage was by contractual arrangements between the principals themselves or their respective sets of kinfolk (e.g., their parents, the senior members of their clans, etc.) or both. Moreover, such contracts always involved exchanges between the parties. In the first place, marriages everywhere required direct, more or less balanced exchange of services (sexual, reproductive, subsistence, protective, etc.) between husband and wife. Moreover, marriages in most places also required exchange of goods between relatives of the principals: of services for services, of objects for services, and/or of objects for objects.

The most common kind of service-for-service exchange involved women themselves, not as chattels but as "bundles" of services (e.g., sexual, reproductive, domestic-labor, and so forth). In some societies such wife exchange was explicit, direct, and simultaneous (e.g., one groom's sister for the other's); in others it was implicit, indirect, and delayed (e.g., in the case of two regularly wife-exchanging clans or three or more clans involved in a wife-giving, wife-receiving circuit). (It should be added that in most cases of wife-for-wife exchange, some objects, such as meals, live pigs, shell valuables, fine mats, etc., were also transferred.)

Marriage exchanges featuring objects for services were of two types: those, technically labeled bride price, in which the bulk of the objects was supplied by the side of the husband, and those where the reverse took place, technically labeled dowry. Bride price was much more common than dowry; in Melanesia especially it sometimes comprised very large amounts of goods (e.g., pigs, shell valuables) and hence required loans and gifts to the groom from his relatives and friends. As many ethnographers have noted, the "price" paid for a bride was usually for her sexual, domestic, and reproductive services; in very few societies was it regarded as payment for her as chattel. Moreover, in some places the payments were on occasion so large (so much larger than normally required there) that their rationale was clearly political (i.e., a means to demonstrate the payers', or rather donors' superiority vis-à-vis the donees).

Turning now to transactions of the objects-for-objects type, we see that some (as in Samoa) involved objects associated with males (e.g., weapons, fishing tackle) exchanged for those associated with females (e.g., fine mats), but in most societies featuring this kind of marital transaction the objects exchanged were the same kind (mainly food, usually in the form of feasts). Although equivalence was the ideal behind most object-for-object marital exchanges, the parties sometimes attempted to gain political advantage by giving more than they received.

Reference was made earlier to the matter of spouse choice: from what categories of persons an Islander could, or could not, choose his wife. (Corresponding rules, of course, applied to females as well, but are phrased here in terms of the male, by whom [or his relatives] the specific selection was most commonly made.) I earlier referred to the nuclear-family incest zone within which all sexual relations, including marriage, were prohibited. (That is, except in Hawaii, where marriage between brother and sister was permitted in chiefly families as a means of enhancing the measure of "divinity" passed on to their progeny.) My earlier reference also went on to state that such prohibitions were in most societies extended to include all relatives classified as "mothers" and "sisters" (e.g., all female clanmates of one's own mother and sister). Regarding the latter, most of the societies of Melanesia and Micronesia were divided into clans that were exogamous (i.e., into common-descent units whose members were forbidden to marry one another). In other societies, especially Polynesian, where common-descent units were not exogamous or in societies where common-descent units did not exist, the most common kind of rule governing choice of spouse was kinship distance (i.e., one ought not to marry any consanguine closer than, say, third cousins, on either father's or mother's side). (Further to the Hawaiian case just mentioned, although marriage between closer kin was permitted in some of the more highly class-stratified societies of Polynesia, such exceptions were usually limited to members of the upper classes.)

Further discussion of kin-based spouse choice will be postponed to chapter 4, where kinship in general, and kin groups in particular, will be systematically described. But before proceeding to other aspects of Island marriage it is important to add that in many Pacific Island societies kinship served also to identify whom one *ought* to marry, as well. Thus, in several of those that were divided into matrilineal clans (i.e., those in which membership devolved through females) a male's preferred, or even prescribed, wife was a daughter of his mother's brother, or one of that daughter's clan "sisters."

Having previously mentioned other wife-choosing criteria such as relative age, comeliness, industriousness, and social class, I pass on to the topic of weddings (i.e., the kind of ceremony that served to unite Islanders in marriage).

In this institution also, Island societies varied widely: from no ceremony at all (except perhaps for that signaling the move of one of the affianced couple into the other's household, in some cases years before sexual cohabitation commenced), to large public gatherings accompanied by feasting and religious rites. But even in societies where elaborate nuptial ceremonies took place, they did not include an exchange of verbal vows between bride and groom. Instead, the new relationship usually began either with an act of eating together or of sexual intercourse, in some societies in planned privacy, in others within the sight or hearing of guests. Further to the latter, among some peoples, such as the Samoans, who attributed high value to a bride's virginity, the weddings of chiefly couples were preceded by (and contingent upon) the manual testing, often public, of a bride's virginity.

Another significant aspect of Islanders' marriages had to do with where the couple resided, a circumstance that reflected and served to shape other aspects of a society's culture, and that in many places was set by conventions, in some cases hard-and-fast rules. If both spouses had previously resided in the same community and continued to reside there, the logical possibilities were as follows: they could after marriage reside either virilocally (i.e.,in the household of the husband), or uxorilocally (in that of the wife), or bilocally (part-time in each), or neolocally (in one where neither had previously resided). Or, if they had previously resided in different communities, the same logical possibilities with reference to community, would have obtained.

In most Island societies the most common pattern of marital residence was virilocal. Even among some societies divided into matrilineal clans patterns of marital residence were bilocal or even virilocal. In other words, matrilineality in descent-unit membership did not necessarily result in uxorilocality, no more than it did in matriarchy (i.e., *rule* by women).

It would require scores of pages to generalize accurately about husband-wife relations in the hundreds of Island societies. Suffice it to say that a division of labor in household matters, and corresponding spheres of authority, obtained in every society, but it was not exactly the same in any two of them. And one must not infer, from men's usual control over most public matters, that they exercised authority over all family and household matters as well. However, instead of attempting to document this caveat I will add a few sentences about two other aspects of Island marriages, namely, secondary marital unions, and divorce.

I know of no Island societies in which there were social or religious sanctions against polygyny (i.e., one husband, more than one wife); indeed, there were some in which it was judged to be enviable. In most of them, however, polygyny per se was neither admired nor (as noted) censured, but was practiced for reasons that were mainly practical or to carry out kinship obligations. An appetite for new and younger sex partners may have reinforced other reasons a man had for acquiring additional wives, but in most places a man did not have to marry to engage in sex. Concerning the practical reasons, there were doubtless situations in which the husband of, say, a barren or sick or decrepit wife required a second one to obtain progeny or to produce enough food for his household. Otherwise, most men were moved to acquire one or more additional wives for reasons that were largely political (e.g., a desire to produce more food, including pigs, for politically enhancing feasting or gift giving, or a wish for the political alliances that would accompany new marital ties). As for the kinship obligations underlying some marriages, mention was made of them earlier in this section, when describing the practice of levirate.

Polyandry (one wife, more than one husband) was practiced "officially" in only one Island society, that of the Marquesas, and even there the status of a secondary husband, a *pekio,* seems not to have been as privileged as that of the *ahana tuia,* or primary one.

Finally, a few words on Islanders' customs regarding divorce. Mercifully, only a very few words are needed, for, in contrast to their many different ways of marrying, their ways of unmarrying were not only simple but nearly everywhere the same, namely, by exit of one or the other of the pair. Reasons for divorce differed both within and between societies, but in substance and in range did not differ markedly from those occurring in other regions of the world.

GROWING OLD

The generally more salubrious natural environments of Polynesia and Micronesia enabled their inhabitants to live longer, on the average, than those of more disease-ridden Melanesia. Also, it is reasonable to assume that there were corresponding differences in the age onset of the inhabitants' physical decline as well. But, as mentioned earlier, Islanders did not reckon age in years or other fixed periods; they judged individuals to be old by other criteria, which, not surprisingly, were not everywhere the same. Physical decrepitude doubtless figured everywhere as a criterion, but was not the only one, nor were all peoples' definitions of decrepitude the same. In some societies, for example, a man was considered old when no longer able to climb a coconut palm, or paddle long distances, or carry heavy logs. On the other hand, in some other societies such activities were specifically assigned to young men, and men adjudged to be old by other criteria (such as wisdom displayed in deliberations) were not even expected to climb palms, etc.

However, lest the preceding sentence be taken to mean that old age, as locally defined, was everywhere associated with wisdom or other attributes deserving respect, it must be stated that that was by no means the case. Even among peoples as culturally alike, in many respects, as those speaking Polynesian languages, the conventional treatment of individuals deemed old varied from obedience and deep respect (e.g., in Pukapuka) to contemptuous disregard and cruel neglect (as in Tahiti).

The places of old women in Island societies seem not to have varied so widely as those of men. Among some peoples they were disvalued as

basely as were old men (but then, they had less distance to fall!). In perhaps most societies, however, they tended to rise somewhat in social
esteem when old, not so much as old *females* but, because of their diminished femaleness, as being more like males.

DEATH—AND BEYOND

Pacific Islanders conceptualized and solemnized death far more than any
other event in an individual's existence. Moreover, some common themes
are discernable in virtually every society's death beliefs and practices, but
not, of course, in their elaboration.

To begin with, it was widely believed that the origin of human dying
had been due to some human action. Previously, many peoples believed,
humans had lived perpetually or been reborn regularly, but that one of
them, either on his own or with spirit intervention, had brought about
permanent mortality, deliberately or accidentally, through actions that
were in many cases ridiculously trivial.

Another widespread belief was that death, once originated, usually
happened to individuals as result of something happening to their soul(s),
either through natural aging (which, for example, loosened the soul's
attachment to the body) or through external spirit intervention (e.g.,
human-directed sorcery, violation of a spirit-sanctioned rule, etc.). Even
instances of sudden death, by accident or in battle, were typically
believed to be the result of, say, a spirit-directed misstep or a spirit-
guided spear. In any event, whatever the specific cause believed to have
brought about an individual's death, his soul (or in some cases, souls)
always left the body and continued to exist for some period of time. But
before listing the several different sets of beliefs regarding a soul's post-
mortem existence, let me summarize what Islanders did in relation to an
individual's dying, and then dead, body.

In perhaps most Island societies efforts were made up to the end to
keep nonsenile but ailing persons alive, by practical or religious measures
(a distinction ofttimes difficult to draw). On the other hand, it was common practice in many places to accept certain locally defined omens as so
decisively fateful that little or nothing was done to ward off death or, in
some cases, actions were deliberately taken to hasten it (e.g., by aban-
donment or even burial alive).

When death finally occurred (or rather, when it was perceived to have
occurred), all Island peoples did one or more of the following things:

First, close relatives of the deceased began to grieve, or intensified their
grieving if, as often happened, they had begun to do so before death.
Some European observers of Islanders' grieving have distinguished
two kinds: "real" (e.g., wild sobbing, self-mortification) and "simulated"

(e.g., patterned sing-song keening). It is doubtless true that the grievers on any particular occasion differed in the profundity of their emotions, but that is not to say that simulated grieving was necessarily a sign of shallow emotions. In fact, every Island people had its own conventional, role-associated pattern of grieving, and one that was not necessarily expressive of depth of feeling. Nor was grief behavior limited to weeping. In many societies it was expressed, for example, by cutting one's hair—or letting it grow; by donning ragged garments; by daubing oneself with mud or pigments (usually black or white); or by acts of self-mortification such as lacerating the body, cutting off a finger, knocking out a tooth, or even suicide. In addition, in nearly every Island society certain relatives of the deceased were required to express their grief by some form of abstinence, such as fasting and sexual continence.

For most of a deceased's relatives, public grieving was quite brief, but for others its sequel, mourning, lasted in some societies for a year or more. The most usual person required to mourn was the surviving spouse, especially, but not solely, the widow. One of the most stringent examples of such practices prevailed in the Trobriand Islands, where a widow was confined in a small dark hut for up to 2 years, never leaving (not even to defecate), smeared with grease and soot, and hand-fed by others. In contrast, the only mourning expected of a widow in Kapauku (western New Guinea) was to act sad for a short while and refrain from remarrying for ten whole days!

Second, relatives of the deceased took steps to remove the released soul, now in most societies a ghost, from the immediate vicinity and, in many cases, to send it on its way. Such steps were mainly religious (e.g., threatening gestures, prayers, and offerings), magical measures to assist the ghost on its journey, and the grieving behavior itself (i.e., its demonstration to the ghost that the grievers were truly sorrow-stricken and hence deserving of its goodwill).

Third, close relatives distanced themselves from some things associated with the deceased: for example, by destroying or magically fumigating his dwelling, garments, tools, and so forth or, more drastically, by moving to another location; by lustral bathing; or by not using his name. Conversely, in many societies survivors attempted to remain close to the deceased by, for example, assuming his name, retaining one of his bones, etc. And in some other societies the survivors did both of these kinds of things: a contradiction, perhaps, to most Europeans but not, it seems, to those Islanders themselves.

Fourth, the survivors took steps to minimize the repellent qualities of the corpse. In some places the odors of decomposition were ignored, but in other places efforts were made to counteract them (e.g., by coating the corpse with scented oil, defleshing its skeleton, etc., or by speedy cremation or burial).

Fifth, they extended the circle of grievers by holding a funeral, which other than close relatives attended, and were in due course compensated for their grieving services, mainly with food. Although the rites carried out at funerals were mainly and explicitly religious, most funerals were implicitly social, and some even political, affairs. Indeed, in many societies more people assembled for funerals than for any other kind of event. Especially when the deceased was an important man, his supporters and successors used the occasion to maintain his (and their) political influence by hyperbolic shows of grief and by lavish display of wealth, manifested mainly in the form of gifts to principal guests. In fact, this genre of social gathering was so useful in maintaining or competing for political influence that in some societies it was periodically repeated, in the form of memorial feasts for long-dead leaders.

Sixth, the surviving relatives of most deceased persons took steps to discover the causes of their deaths and, if feasible, to avenge them or to minimize chances of repetition. Referring to the causes, listed earlier, it is noteworthy, and not surprising, that there were differences in such findings. In Polynesia, for example, the causes were attributed mainly to direct spirit intervention, in Micronesia mainly to natural aging or pure accident (i.e., with no spirit intervention), and in most of Melanesia mainly to spirits acting independently or with human manipulation (i.e., sorcery). Such having been the case, there were corresponding differences in the steps taken to counter death (e.g., in Polynesia largely expiatory sacrifice, in Melanesia largely countersorcery).

Seventh, and finally, every Island people eventually took steps to remove the corpse, or what remained of the corpse, from the mundane scene. In some societies this was done by cremation, in others by sea burial, but in most by burial on land, the latter in many cases having been done in stages (e.g., a preliminary installation of the whole corpse on a bier, followed by final burial of its bones in the ground). In most societies the final disposition of corpses was done within days or even hours of death; in others (i.e., mostly where it was done in stages) final disposition occurred only after months or even years.

We turn now to beliefs concerning the fates experienced by souls after they left their mortals' dead bodies. In some societies a death-released soul remained the same in name; in others it was renamed, having become a different kind of spirit, a "ghost" (the label I shall use here). But before proceeding it should be stated that Islanders' beliefs about afterlife ranged in content from unconnected bits and pieces of guesses, associated with widespread disinterest, to elaborate and detailed collections of tenets enjoying deep public interest and concern. It must be added, however, that except in the case of very small societies (such as one-community ones) there were no unified "official" collections of beliefs in any of them regarding the fates of ghosts (nor indeed about any other domain of religious belief). Moreover, in the case of many written descriptions about Islanders' religious beliefs, the comprehensiveness and systematics attributed to them usually turn out to be the result of the writers' mistaken efforts to "tidy up" and synthesize the, typically, disparate, raw facts. With these cautions in mind, let us list some of the many kinds of beliefs, held by this or that set of persons, in one or another Island society, about the fates of ghosts and about their actions towards mortals. First, where did ghosts reside?

In the beliefs of some Islanders, ghosts remained permanently (or rather, until they were forgotten) near their mortals' abodes; in most cases, however, it was believed that they went to some other place or places, from which some of them returned occasionally to their previous earthly communities. Opinions differed widely concerning the locations and characteristics of those places. Among some peoples, interest in an Afterworld was so slight that individuals expressed ignorance of the matter or described its location simply as "somewhere else." At the opposite pole were societies whose members (or at least the more "learned" of its members) conceived of an Afterworld (commonly conceptualized as a general abode of all types of spirits) in very detailed terms, including in many cases more than one (e.g., a Heaven and a Hell; or a Heaven, a Purgatory, and a Hell). In addition, some of the more elaborate doctrines included specifics regarding the journey of the ghosts en route, which in many instances was perilous and contained episodes in which the novice ghost was adjudged by a deity and assigned to one or the other of the Afterworld's domains.

In the beliefs of some peoples a ghost was assigned to a fate, either pleasant or painful, according to the social-ethical behavior of its mortal person; in most, however, the latter's earthly behavior towards fellow mortals had little or no effect upon its Afterworld fate. More often, the assignment was made to correspond with the social status of the mortal or according to its religious behavior. Thus, in some societies a person whose death had led his heirs and associates to expend large amounts on his funeral or one who had been extra generous in offerings to spirits was believed to be rewarded with residence in a Paradise, whereas a mortal of little earthly influence, etc., was assigned to his society's version of Hell. Or, there were some other sets of beliefs in which a ghost's fate was assigned on a basis of chance so arbitrary and otherwise trivial as to defy explanation by any logic that I know of.

Finally, Island peoples differed in their views concerning ghosts' dispositions towards mortal mankind. Some viewed them to be uniformly benevolent, others to be uniformly malevolent, and still others benevolent or malevolent, according to circumstances or according to each ghost's prior way of living or manner of dying. (For example, the soul of a generous mortal became a generous ghost; the soul of a man killed in battle a vengeful one.) Still another variation was the belief entertained in some societies that a person had two souls and hence two ghosts, one of them friendly, the other hostile. And adding another dimension to all the above, Island peoples differed widely with respect to the amount of human interaction attributed to their ghosts, from very frequent (almost daily) to virtually none.

FIGHTING

Islanders on the average spent far less time trying to harm one another physically than, say, gardening and fishing, but for many of them injuring, even killing, other humans occupied a large amount of their thinking and influenced many other things that they did. In summarizing how they went about injuring (or killing), I will distinguish between their military and their religious methods (i.e., between direct assault on a victim's body by clubs, spears, etc., and measures aimed at injuring a person by attacks on his soul, etc.). ("Military" is not entirely apt for the meaning intended, but is the nearest term I can think of. Also, for many Islanders the above distinction would likely have been less sharp than this exposition seems to suggest, but that is an intrinsic hazard of translating one's own cultural concepts into another's.) But before listing those methods, something should be said about what induced Islanders to try to injure or kill. The reference here is not to such allegedly pan-human propensities as xenophobia or fighting instincts, and not to idiosyncratic reasons such as hidden jealousies or thwarted sexual advances, but to those kinds of situations and events that prompted persons to unite to injure or kill, or that were recognized by a whole community as sufficient grounds for doing so.

Causes

The most widespread and impelling reason that led Islanders to try to injure or kill one another was to avenge real or imagined wrongs committed against themselves or (and this is important) other members of their social units (however such persons happened to be identified). The wrongs regarded as outrageous enough to warrant lethal revenge differed somewhat from society to society, but in one place or another included killing, serious bodily injury, abduction or seduction of females, theft, and insult.

In many societies members killed outsiders, even without specific provocation, as a way of enhancing their social status (having afterwards commonly exhibited some part of the victim's body as proof of the deed). Such acts were in some cases performed by individuals for self-glorification, in other cases by one community against another for political aggrandizement, with or without accompanying material spoils.

Some motives that led many Islanders to kill can be labeled economic. Everyday food was seldom if ever an object, but a few peoples (including Fijians and some New Guineans) did raid nearby communities for human flesh. More often, raids were undertaken to secure live humans to serve as laborers or sexual partners. Land was also the object of raiding, including killing, in some places, but mostly by groups of persons who had themselves been dispossessed. But far more frequent were raids carried out to obtain transferrable valuables, such as pigs and shell money.

Religion was a factor in most of the above (e.g., in status-enhancing head-hunting), but in some societies religious motives were the primary ones for killing, as, for example, in the Marquesas, where scores of persons ("human fish") were kidnapped each year for sacrifice to the gods (and then ceremonially eaten by their captors). Another convention of religiously motivated killing was the widespread practice of killing trespassers upon forbidden scenes (e.g., females catching sight of men's sacred flutes, unauthorized persons trespassing, even innocently, into sacred precincts).

Finally, anyone who has read widely in the ethnography and early postcontact history of this region will probably agree that some members of many of its societies engaged in lethal fighting for the sheer pleasure of doing so, a conclusion that will be confirmed a little later in the mention of the gamelike nature of much intercommunity fighting.

"Military" Fighting

The most widely used offensive weapons of the Islanders were spears, clubs, axes, and bows and arrows (Fig. 3.5). Of more limited distribution were sling stones (mainly in eastern Polynesia), daggers, swords, cutting rasps, knuckle-dusters, strangling cords, and tripping cords. Although bows and arrows served as weapons in Melanesia, throughout much of Polynesia they were, inexplicably, used only for hunting or sport.

Reports agree upon the deadly accuracy of Islanders' use of slings but are less approving about their effectiveness with arrows and throwing spears (the former having been unfeathered). In fact, most serious combative fighting was accomplished with cutting, jabbing, and striking weapons, in particular, clubs and axes.

Weapons training per se took place in only a few societies; because most of the kinds of implements used as weapons served also, indeed mainly, in ordinary occupations, practice in using them was a part of a male's everyday life. More so than with ordinary implements, however, Islanders sought to empower their weapons religiously, with magic, sup-

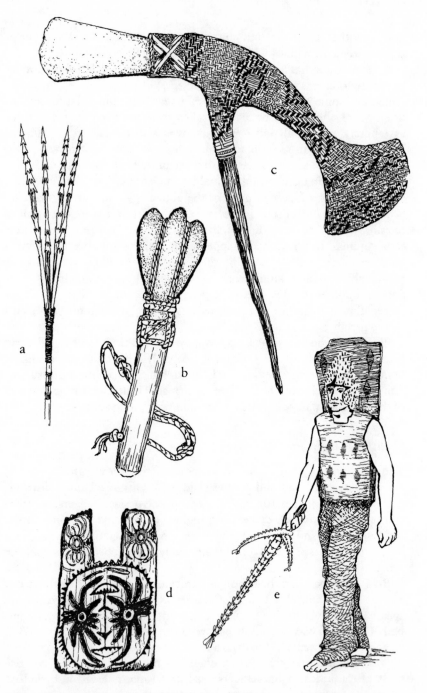

Figure 3.5. Implements for fighting: *a,* wooden spear head, Fiji; *b,* stone-headed club, Hawaii; *c,* ax, New Guinea Highlands; *d,* shield, Purari Delta, Gulf of Papua, New Guinea; *e,* man in armor, Gilbert Islands

plication, and offering. In addition, when engaged in mass combat it was customary in many societies for the fighters to try to terrify and thereby weaken their enemies by means of fierce-looking body painting and intimidating shouts and gestures.

The only weapons used exclusively for defense were shields, and those in only a few places. Instead, reliance was placed on dodging (in which some men were highly adept), on parrying (with clubs, spears, and axes), on protective garments (in many societies, helmets; in a few, cord-plaited armor), and, of course, on magic and other religious measures.

To the above must also be added the measures employed by Islanders to defend their residences from both open and secret attack. In many societies whole communities were located, deliberately, in defensible locations or houses were constructed in defensible ways. And in a few (e.g., Fiji and New Zealand) whole communities were built in or near palisaded forts and encircled by camouflaged traps. In addition, a few societies, mainly in Polynesia, contained institutionalized places of refuge, where innocent bystanders (and sometimes defeated warriors) could find asylum in times of general warfare.

An exhaustive study of military fighting among Pacific Islanders would conceivably reveal there to have been a score or so of types, ranging from murder and assassination within a community to pitched battles between two communities or federations of communities, and including intracommunity brawls, raids, ambushes, sieges, etc. But even a random sampling of ethnographies indicates that Island peoples differed with respect to the types they engaged in and their rules, or lack of rules, for doing so. Thus, the New Guinea Dani, whose multi-person fighting persisted until recently and was witnessed by anthropologists, distinguished five types: brawls (within communities or confederations of communities and usually between individuals supported by their relatives); feuds (also within confederations and, although at times bloody, often settled by compensation); raids (usually by small parties acting secretly); periodic open, seesaw battles between confederations, which were conducted with such constraint and ritual as to resemble sporting events; and all-out battles of extermination. Some other societies favored ambushing, still others total extermination (as distinct from mere property destruction or kidnapping) raids. And although secret, often treacherous, raiding was perhaps the most popular type of fighting throughout the Islands, it must be added that sportive warfare was also very widespread.

A comparative study of Island intercommunity fighting (i.e., warfare) would likely reveal some association between the types practiced and such other factors as physical environment, population density, and social organization. Thus, it makes sense, for example, for a thinly scattered, forest-dwelling people led by successful headhunters (such as the New Guinea Asmat) to practice mainly ambushing and small-party raiding; and for a populous, shore-dwelling, autocratically governed community (such as Borabora) to specialize in large-scale naval raiding and pitched battles fought at sea.

Some fighting between Island communities ended in the extermination or displacement or assimilation of the vanquished. In many more cases it went on perpetually, in the form of battles that were evenly matched, back-and-forth affairs. On the other hand, some stalemated conflicts were mutually terminated by the combatants to the accompaniment of peace ceremonies, which, however, usually proved to be even less binding over time than those between modern nations.

We turn next to the religious aspects of military fighting. Mention has already been made of some religious causes of such killing and of the use of magic and of direct spirit intervention in the empowering of weapons. Spirits also figured in decisions as to whether and when to engage in military fighting, especially in intercommunity combat; their views were communicated through dreams, omens, auguries, and human mediums. Thus, in New Zealand, mistakes made by warriors in prebattle dancing were taken to be signs of possible defeat, which in many instances led to postponement of those particular wars. Also, spirits were appealed to, not only to empower individual weapons, but to render enemies less skillful or more vulnerable, or even to "prekill" them (mainly through magic designed to destroy or remove their souls). And among the many kinds of defensive religious measures undertaken was one whereby warriors setting off to battle left their souls at home, beyond the reach of enemy weapons and magic.

Victory in fighting was followed nearly everywhere by religious thank-offerings (in some societies by sacrifice of captured enemies). And defeat was commonly viewed by the vanquished as punishment for "sins," of commission or omission, and therefore requiring expiatory prayers and offerings.

Finally, although I know of no religion-based ethical principles that served to prohibit or terminate intercommunity fighting, it was the convention in some societies to interrupt fighting while unrelated, religious ceremonies were taking place.

Religious Fighting

As just described, Islanders' efforts to injure or kill one another by what Europeans might call physical or military means made use of various religious measures as well. In addition, there were many occasions on which they relied entirely or mainly on the latter to kill or physically injure persons toward whom they felt hostile. And although religious measures were at times directed toward two or more persons simultaneously, most of them involved only one victim at a time.

Here is a list of the kinds of religious techniques employed by Islanders to kill or physically injure one another (not all of them were practiced in every Island society, and none of them was distinctive of the Islands):

1. Spirit invocation: direct petitions to spirits by words or other actions, asking them to kill the intended victim;
2. Telepathy: killing by means of wishing alone;
3. Witchcraft: engaging in direct personal attack on the victim by means of special inherent powers of maleficence;
4. Bespelling: use of inherently potent words or other actions;
5. Poison: causing the victim to ingest or otherwise come into physical contact with some substance that was "poisonous," either naturally or religiously so;
6. Projectile: impelling a religiously deadly object at the victim from a distance;
7. Effigy: making an image or portrait of the victim and attacking it with deadly means;
8. Bait: obtaining something physically identified with the victim and attacking it with deadly means; and
9. Assault: rendering the victim unconscious, then removing some vital organ (e.g., blood, soul, kidney) or emplacing some lethal object, such as a bamboo splinter, in him, then restoring him to normal appearance but to mental vacancy, and swift death.

Although actual use of any of the above measures probably did not take place as often as Islanders imagined, most deaths, and illnesses and serious accidents, seem to have been attributed to such causes. That having been the case, most deaths (that is, except of the very old and, perhaps, of the very young) moved survivors to discover the particular (religious) cause and if appropriate to redress it (by religious countermeasures or by direct physical action). In some societies this required separate acts of autopsy, inquest, and retaliation by three separate specialists; in others all three were combined and carried out by one "generalist" magician.

Belief in the effectiveness of religious killing encouraged Islanders to defend themselves against it. For example, most of them sought to avoid places where potential killers, human or spirit, were believed to lurk, particularly in territories outside one's own and virtually everywhere outside after dark. Another widespread defense was to arm oneself with protective magic; still another was to keep one's own waste matter (hair cuttings, cast-off garments, body excretions, food leavings, etc.) out of the reach of persons who might use it as magical bait. It should not be concluded, however, that Islanders lived in a continual state of fear as a result of their belief in the reality of religious killing (no more so than

Americans do of being struck by automobiles), but they did take steps to reduce the risks and thereby doubtless reduced the fear.

EXCHANGING

Harking back to the labels for social units used in this book, community is the one given to a distinct cluster of households whose members shared enough sentiments of unity, and of difference from nonmembers, to dispose them to interact among themselves in relatively peaceful and cooperative ways and to settle disputes among themselves by means short of unbridled killing. A society, on the other hand, is herein defined as a unit composed of persons who shared, distinctively, a common culture, including usually a common language. (Most societies consisted of more than one community.)

As will be described in chapter 4, in only a few places were two or more Island communities joined together for long periods into unitary political units. Elsewhere, relations between adjacent communities, including those of the same society, were, at worst, perennially and lethally hostile and, at best, traditionally peaceful and occasionally friendly but always wary. The kind of activity that was most effective in maintaining the latter state of affairs, and in interrupting and mitigating the former, was exchange.

Amicable relations between humans are in some cases created and maintained by one-way giving (as for example between a parent and young child), but most such relations depend upon exchange, that is, two-way transfer of goods (objects or services), of which there are two types, direct and indirect. The latter, best characterized as pool-sharing, was the way in which most Island household economies worked; each member contributed certain conventionally defined kinds and amounts of goods to a common "pool" (e.g., from a wife: garden weeding, cooking, and infant care; from a husband: garden-site clearing, firewood collecting, and roof mending; from a son: fish; from a daughter: house cleaning) and removed from it conventionally defined kinds and amounts of goods (e.g., cooked food, shelter, etc.). The maxim was: From each according to his (conventionally defined) resources, to each according to his (conventionally defined) needs. In many Island societies pool-sharing also occurred at the community level of organization: for example, when residents presented food to their leader, who in return led them in battle or represented them in petitions to the community's tutelar spirits. But most transactions among community members were in the form of direct exchange.

In contrast to pool-sharing, direct exchange consists of a transfer of something (an object or a service) directly from A to B, with the expectation that something of equivalent value will be received in return. Barter and buying and selling are self-evident examples of direct exchange, but there are several other less explicit kinds: for example, the exchange, over time, of services between friends; a parent's support of an adolescent child, based on (conventional) expectation of eventual repayment (this in contrast to the nature of one-way giving that takes place between parent and younger children). Even less explicit is a kind of direct exchange that *pretends* to be one-way giving but implicitly requires eventual repayment (e.g., the type of dinner-party "giving" that prevails among peers in American middle-class circles).

Direct-exchanging was the most common cement of social relationships among Pacific Islanders (as indeed among humans everywhere). Within single communities it occurred alongside one-way giving and pool-sharing; between members of separate communities, however, except for fighting, direct-exchanging was the most usual form of interaction, of which there were several varieties.

One way of discriminating between varieties of direct-exchanging concerns its purpose; namely, was it engaged in mainly to obtain the transferred goods, or to establish or sustain or transform a social relationship between the exchangers? (Many direct exchanges between communities doubtless had both purposes, but more usually one or the other was paramount.) Other ways of discriminating varieties of direct-exchanging included the amount of haggling that accompanied it, the degree to which it was monetized, the presence or absence of ceremony, the time elapsed between the transfers, and the social setting of the exchanging. Let me exemplify.

The most unambiguous form of goods-focused exchange was "silent trade," a form of barter in which, for example, residents of inland communities exchanged their vegetables and forest products for fish from nearby shore-dwellers with whom their relations were too hostile to permit face-to-face barter. In such situations, one party deposited its wares at some traditional place on a customary day and then withdrew, whereupon the other party collected those wares, deposited theirs, and then went home, leaving their counterparts to collect them. The sanctions that kept such exchanging going were the mutual desire for the goods bartered and the knowledge that the other party would discontinue bartering if its members judged the proffered goods unequivalent in value. However, not all exchanging between communities with different resources was silent; in many more cases it took place at fixed marketplaces, where the barterers, or buyers and sellers, intermingled, and where attitudes ranged from touch-and-go hostility to (temporary) amicability.

Goods-focused exchanging also took place between widely separated communities, one example of such having been the *hiri* trade of the Gulf of Papua. Once a year, about twenty of the thirty-man sailing rafts (*laka-toi*) of the Motu-speaking people (who lived near the present town of Port Moresby) traveled 150 or more miles west to barter their locally manufactured pots for sago produced by peoples of the Vailala and Purari deltas. All the boats traveled at about the same time, but each one from a different village and each to a separate destination (which was usually the same year after year). Then, some weeks later, after the winds had shifted eastwards, the visitors returned home laden with sago and other goods. Although each boat was manned by members of a single Motu community, it was not community property. Rather, it was owned by one or another of the community's ambitious members, whose sponsorship of an expedition served to enhance his local prestige. Moreover, each member of the expedition traded separately, both for himself and as agent for relatives back home.

Another variety of goods-focused exchange was to be found in North-Central New Guinea, in the area between the Sepik River and the coast. This area comprised three sharply distinct geographic zones, rolling grasslands, mountains, and coastal plains, each having different natural resources and each producing some distinctive goods wanted by the others. These goods passed from zone to zone in two different ways: by small parties of traveling barterers, and by individuals in one zone making gifts (i.e., gift-exchanges) to their exchange partners in the adjacent zone (partnerships having become hereditary over time).

Still another variety of goods-focused exchanging depended upon the services of middlemen. A large-scale example of that took place in the vicinity of New Guinea's Vitiaz Strait, encompassing an area about 180 miles long and 60 wide. This area included many different natural environments (e.g., inland mountains, plains, coastal strips, small offshore islands), numerous peoples, and many kinds of natural and manufactured trade objects. Within the area there were also numerous local trade zones, zones within which adjacent communities exchanged local products by barter or gift-exchange. In addition, the whole area was drawn together through the activities of Siassi Island middlemen, who traveled regularly in their large canoes to all coastal communities in the area, bartering goods. Two of their four home islands were not even large enough to supply their residents with vegetables, which they obtained by barter, for fish, from nearby islands. But even those nearby islands were unable to provide some of the Siassi with the pigs they needed to engage in the competitive feasting that was their means for acquiring and maintaining local social esteem and political influence. To acquire those pigs they had to go far afield. The communities with surplus pigs happened not to want Siassi products (i.e., mats and coconuts), so the traders had to go elsewhere to barter their home products for pots, to another place to exchange the pots for wooden bowls, and finally to other places to exchange the bowls for pigs. To do all this they sailed their outrigger canoes up and down the Strait twice a year. And in doing so they not only acquired the pigs they themselves needed, but served to circulate goods throughout the whole area, including within the many local trade zones, whose exchanges were thereby diversified and accelerated.

Similar goods-focused, middlemen-serviced networks existed in and around New Guinea (e.g., within the Admiralty Islands, in the Huon Gulf, and along the eastern part of the Papuan Gulf). As in the Vitiaz Strait network, many of the goods exchanged within them originated in and ended up in communities far beyond the coastal entrepôt visited by the voyaging middlemen. Also as in the Vitiaz network, although the main purpose of most of the myriad exchanges was commercial (i.e., to obtain the goods themselves) many of them took place through established trade partnerships, an institution that requires some clarification, but after a few observations about "money."

Some writers consider the term "money" inappropriate for the objects so called in descriptions of many Pacific Island transactions, pointing out that in most such cases those objects served other purposes as well, and that they could not be used to buy as many kinds of objects and services as can the money used in modern market-exchange economies. Although it is true, as those critics charge, that the "money" used in Islanders' exchanges could not buy as many kinds of objects and services as, say, a dollar or a franc or a yen, that difference is a matter of degree. (Even in modern economies some things are "priceless.") And although, as also charged, some Island "money" was also used for other purposes (e.g., for ornamentation and heirlooms), parallels of that can be found in modern economies as well.

In this connection, however, it should be noted that Island peoples differed widely in their use of money. For example, many Polynesian societies had nothing even remotely similar to multipurpose exchange tokens (i.e., money). In contrast, in many societies in Melanesia money (mainly in the form of shells) was used not only in strictly commercial ways (e.g., in buying food, weapons, and, in some places, concubines), but in many social-relational transactions as well (e.g., paying brideprice, making gifts). An extreme occurred among the Kapauku people of western New Guinea, where the money (shells of different sizes) consisted of several denominations of fixed equivalences, and where it was used to purchase not only objects of nearly every kind, but labor and (a very rare occurrence in Island societies) use-rights in land.

Returning to partnerships: before the colonial era the Siuai people of southwest Bougainville carried on a lively trade with natives of the nearby islands of Alu and Mono, exchanging their pigs, taro, smoked almonds, pottery, decorated spears, and sometimes humans, for the latters' fish, lime for betel chewing, and shell money. Most of this trade was initiated by the peoples of Mono and Alu, who were more maritime and who carried their wares to coastal Siuai communities in their canoes. In the course of time Siuai leaders, both coastal and inland, established formalized trade partnerships (*taovu*) with one or more of the visitors to facilitate trade (including provision of protection for the visiting partners). In addition to this overseas commerce, *taovu* partnerships also existed within Siuai itself.

With the exception of a few items, nearly all Siuai households were materially self-sufficient, but those few items were indispensable enough to encourage interhousehold and intercommunity exchange. One of these items was cooking pots; the average household had to replace about three of them a year, feast-giving leaders up to seven or eight. Pot making was centered in northeastern Siuai, partly because the best clay was located there and partly because it was customary for men in that area to specialize in pot making. But even the most productive potters did not peddle their wares; they manufactured either on commission or with the expectation that purchasers would seek them out. Consequently, most householders in need of pots had to spend some time walking about searching for unoccupied potters or for saleable pots not already promised to other buyers. Thus, men with forethought tried to arrange for a regular source of supply by going to the same potter each time and thereby establishing an informal pot-buying relationship. And the more affluent men came in time to transform that relationship into a formal *taovu* partnership, which in due course led to the exchange between the partners of many other items as well (e.g., lime for betel chewing, almonds, weapons, etc., and especially pigs) and to the mutual lending of money. An active feast-giver would have had up to five or six *taovu* with whom he exchanged visits, small gifts, and so forth, and upon whom he depended very heavily when amassing materials for a feast. In some cases the relationships were so active that the partners' respective communities also became known as *taovu*.

Exchange between *taovu* was verbally distinguished from ordinary barter and purchase, the latter having been called *pu*, the former *ootu* (literally, reciprocal giving). *Taovu*, it was held, ought not to haggle; indeed, when one of them presented something to his partner the latter was expected to reciprocate, eventually, with something of equivalent or, better, more than equivalent value, but not *too* much more.

Partnerships similar to *taovu* existed in many other Island societies, having served to reduce the personal dangers faced by outsiders when trading away from home, to simplify the search for sellers and buyers, and to mitigate the hostilities attending haggling. Most of them were at first means to an end (i.e., to acquire the goods exchanged), but they were in some places regarded as the end itself, which leads to consideration of relationship-focused exchange.

Much of the exchanging that took place *within* Island communities doubtless focused on sustaining or enhancing relationships: between kinsmen, between neighbors, between leader and followers, etc. In many parts of the islands analogous transactions took place between whole communities as well (i.e., between leading members or representatives of communities). And although there were numerous differences among those transactions (in specific purpose, in procedure, in scale, etc.), they were all alike in pretending that the goods exchanged were one-way gifts.

Throughout Polynesia and in much of Micronesia nearly all intercommunity exchanging was of this kind. In fact, in some societies of those areas it was held that barter and other exchanges that were explicitly two-way were ignoble, especially if haggling was involved. Some writers attribute that attitude to the peoples' lack of need for two-way exchanging, due to the sameness of goods produced in all communities within exchanging reach (i.e., in contrast to the sharply different natural settings, and hence goods, that obtained throughout much of Melanesia). Be that as it may, throughout Polynesia and much of Micronesia the ethos underlying gift-exchanging was most commonly expressed in acts of hospitality, in "giving" food and other valued objects and services (e.g., entertainment) to visitors from other communities.

Events involving hospitality, both small-scale and large, occurred also in Melanesia, but gift-exchange institutions existed there in other forms as well. One example was to be found among the Siuai of Bougainville, whose trade-partner institution was just described. Those partnerships were clearly goods-focused in inception although the partners in them were regarded as friendly equals and, as noted, the exchanges between them were distinguished from ordinary bartering and buying and selling. Different again were a set of exchanges that culminated in one known as "*mumi* honoring."

The core members of nearly every Siuai community belonged to the same (matrilineal) clan, who owned in common the land on which they resided and gardened, and who respected the wishes of their eldest clanmates, their male and female Firstborns, in matters respecting their land and other clan property (including the heirloom shell money that was used in members' marital exchanges). In addition, in many communities there were one or two men known as *mumi* (now translated in pidgin as "Big-man"), who were not necessarily Firstborns and whose activities, and consequent influence, extended beyond clan matters. Those activities consisted mainly in giving feasts, not for local consumption, such as in celebration of births and marriages, but for attendance by outsiders. And the larger and more frequent those feasts, the greater became the host's *potu*, his renown: another example of exchange (i.e., the host's food, especially pork, in exchange for the guests' grateful, *potu*-enhancing praise).

Such praise was sweet to the ears of Siuai men, and many of them sought actively for it. Simple liberality, including everyday hospitality, also won social approval, but *potu* was generated only through giving feasts and in a conventional series of steps. First, a would-be *mumi* must have his own clubhouse, an open-sided building located on a well-traveled path at some distance from dwellings and other areas frequented by females (clubhouses were barred to them). Many men inherited clubhouses from fathers or clanmates, but for an owner to derive social credit from its ownership he was required to re-roof or enlarge it, employing some outsiders in doing so and then rewarding their labors with a sumptuous pork feast. The next step in becoming a *mumi* was to install wooden slit-gongs in one's clubhouse or add to those already there. (These hollowed-out sections of tree trunk were beaten on many solemn occasions, including announcing the value of pigs distributed at feasts, a signal known as "renown sounding.") Again, however, for a gong to redound to the renown of its owner, the men who helped to construct and install it had to be rewarded with a sumptuous feast. Thereafter, a would-be *mumi* used every occasion his resources permitted to give feasts, including installing in his clubhouse a demon, which would aid him in his endeavors and protect him from magical attack by envious rivals, and which, with metaphoric aptness, was nourished by the blood of pigs killed for the owner's feasts. (A blood-starved demon would have slain the clubhouse owner.)

After becoming the principal *mumi* of his own community, a man could either relax in his efforts and bask in the local sun of esteem, or he could seek to increase and extend his renown by competing, directly and unequivocally, with *mumi* of other communities near and far. This was done by means of feasts known (with unconscious irony!) as *muminai* (*mumi*-honoring feasts), wherein a host presented to his guest of honor (a rival *mumi*) a "gift" of pigs and shell valuables beyond (the host hoped) the latter's ability to reciprocate, thereby establishing the host's superiority over the latter in this deadly social game (deadly, because it was believed that the loser was not only diminished socially but was injured magically by the host's protective demon). If, however, the "honored" guest was able to reciprocate with a return feast (and accompanying gift) more or less equal in value to the one received, the contest between the two was seen to be a draw, and they thenceforth became equals, even *taovu*. Or, if the original guest wished to continue the contest he answered with a feast, and a gift, much more costly than the one received, and the rivalry continued until one of the pair was defeated, and therefore diminished, or until they balanced the giving and ended up as equals.

On first glimpse this seems to have been nothing more nor less than a contest of wealth, to demonstrate which contestant had more pigs and shell valuables to "give" away. Such wealth was indeed the scrip of the contest, but it was not necessarily, nor even commonly, scrip belonging to the chief players themselves. No Siuai individual was able to accumulate and own outright enough pigs or shell valuables to engage for long in this very costly contest. To accumulate them for specific occasions he had to borrow from relatives and neighbors and *taovu,* in other words to be a persuasive borrower and clever financier.

And what rewards did victory in the status-rivalry contest bring? Certainly, considerable authority in the victor's own community and some advantage elsewhere in buying pigs and in obtaining loans. But despite the fact that even the most successful *mumi* had no political authority beyond his own community, some men spent most of their energies in achieving that status. Evidently, to a Siuai *potu* itself was sufficient reward.

Mumi-like institutions existed in many societies in Melanesia. Those of largest scale were to be found in the Highlands of New Guinea; one of them, the *moka,* involved thousands of persons residing in the vicinity of Mt. Hagen. Another even larger, the *te,* prevailed over an east-west distance of 40–60 miles. And although neither the *moka* nor the *te* nor similar institutions in that and other parts of Melanesia had the effect of eliminating more lethal kinds of intercommunity fighting, they undoubtedly served to interrupt it for shorter or longer periods of time.

I will end this section on intercommunity exchanging with descriptions of two more institutions, both of them of large scale and both having features unlike any of those previously summarized. One has come to be known as *kula,* the other the "Yap Empire."

The *kula* took place in the Massim area, a scattering of islands east of southeastern New Guinea. The numerous peoples of this area engaged in lively intra- and interisland barter in consequence of their many local differences in raw material and craft specialization and by means of their large ocean-going canoes. In addition, many of the islands there were linked in a vast network of exchange whose objects had no economic value in the normal meaning of the word. This was a mode of exchange wherein two types of highly valued shell ornaments (armlets and necklaces) were kept in more or less continuous circulation, necklaces clockwise and armlets counterclockwise, through a wide ring of islands, by passing from one man in a *kula* partnership to the next. By generally observed conventions, no man could retain a *kula* armlet or necklace for more than about a year nor pass it back in the direction from which it was received. Every *kula* participant had at least two partners, one clockwise of him, the other counterclockwise; most men had several in both directions, from whom they regularly received and to whom they regularly "gave" necklaces or armlets.

Whatever its origin, the continuing stimulus for the *kula* exchange was the pleasure men derived in possessing, even temporarily, those fine rare objects and of course the prestige attached thereto.

The central transaction between *kula* partners consisted of an initial "gift" of an armlet (or necklace) by one partner to another and the eventual reciprocation by the latter of a necklace (or armlet) of equivalent value. (Equivalence was measured in terms of the ornament's size, age, history, craftsmanship, etc., and disagreement over it usually led to an end to the partnership.) In the case of partners living near one another, the return gift was usually made within days or even minutes, but for those living on different islands the return was delayed by up to a year, until, that is, the indebted partner could join with similarly indebted neighbors in an overseas expedition to their creditor-partners' island (which in some cases would be 100 and more miles away).

Overseas *kula* expeditions were grand and laborious undertakings, requiring months of preparation, including construction of new canoes, long and hazardous voyages, much supplementary gift-exchanging, and of course many religious observances (e.g., to guard against sea demons en route, to render one's *kula* partner more liberal). Expedition members took along other objects of everyday utility (e.g., pots, carved wooden bowls, tools), which they exchanged for products of the hosts' island by regular barter, but those exchanges were unmistakably secondary to the primary objective of the expedition, the exchange and temporary possession of nonutilitarian armlets and necklaces.

The last exchange institution to be described took place over an area even larger than the *kula* ring. Every two or three years a fleet of about twenty large canoes visited the island of Yap in the Carolines to engage in several kinds of transactions: to barter, to exchange "gifts," to render religious offerings, and to pay "tribute." The expedition started out from atoll islands 700 miles east of Yap and picked up additional canoeloads from islands along the way. Each canoe represented a single community and carried three kinds of "official" gifts, called Religious Tribute, Canoe Tribute, and Tribute of the Land, along with items for individual "giving" and barter, all consisting of atoll manufactures such as woven fiber skirts and loincloths, coconut-fiber twine, and shell. Upon reaching Yap, the fleet's "admiral" (its highest-ranking clan Senior) presented the combined Religious and Canoe Tributes to the chief of one of Yap's districts, while the representatives of each of the expedition's participating communities passed their own Land Tribute directly to the heads of the Yapese clans who claimed figurative ownership of their respective home islands. After a seasonal change of wind direction, the visitors left for home, carrying counter-"gifts" of Yapese products received from their individual hosts.

In view of the labels attached to the official Tributes and of the deferential manner in which they were presented, the atoll communities that participated in this large affair have come to be known as parts of the

"Yap Empire." And so they were, but in a very peculiar and attenuated way. No one knows how the "empire" originated—certainly not as the outcome of Yapese military conquest. Perhaps it was "invented" by the atoll dwellers, who were from time to time driven to seek refuge on high-island Yap as a result of the hurricanes and tidal waves that made their own low-lying islets untenable for months or even years. Rendering tribute served to ensure their future welcome on Yap in times of need and to satisfy their own ever-present wishes for goods not obtainable on their low and sandy home islands. In any case, as a result of its mutual economic advantages the fiction of "empire" was mutually sustained, even including a commonly held belief that spirits would punish any "colonial" community that failed to pay tribute and rent.

Sources

Domicile: Firth 1936; Green 1970; Labby 1976; Lingenfelter 1975; Ross 1973.

Boats and Ocean Travel: Alkire 1970; Dening 1962; Doran 1976; Finney 1967, 1977; Finney and Houston 1966; Gladwin 1970; Goodenough 1953; Haddon and Hornell 1936–38; Hornell 1970; Levison, Ward, and Webb 1973; Lewis 1972, 1978; Riesenberg 1976; Sharp 1963.

Food: Akamichi 1978; Alkire 1978; Anell 1960; Barrau 1958, 1961, 1965; Brookfield and Hart 1971; Bulmer 1968, 1974; Burton-Bradley 1972; Clarke 1971; Dornstreich 1977; Holmes 1967; Huber 1980; Kirch and Dye 1979; Métraux 1940; Rappaport 1968; Reinman 1967; Titcomb 1969; Townsend 1970; Yen 1973, 1974; Young 1971.

Sex: Danielsson 1956; Davenport 1976; Deacon 1934; Ford 1945; Herdt 1981; Marshall and Suggs 1971; Mead 1930a; Meggitt 1964; Oliver 1974; F. Williams 1936.

Reproduction: M. R. Allen 1967; Malinowski 1932; Schneider 1968.

Marriage: Burrows and Spiro 1953; Firth 1936; Freeman 1983; Handy 1923; Malinowski 1932; Meggitt 1964; Meggitt and Glasse 1969; Oliver 1974; F. Williams 1936.

Growing Old: Beaglehole and Beaglehole 1938; Oliver 1974.

Death—and Beyond: Burrows and Spiro 1953; Fortune 1932; Goodenough 1971; Malinowski 1932; Oliver 1955, 1974; Pospisil 1958; Ross 1973.

Fighting: Alkire 1977; Berndt 1962, 1964; Buck 1957; Chowning and Goodenough 1971; Clunie 1977; Dening 1978; Fortune 1932; Godelier 1982; Grimble 1952; Handy 1927; Heider 1970; Hogbin 1964; Kaberry 1971; Kamakau 1961; Koch 1974; Lawrence and Meggitt 1965; Leenhardt 1930; Lingenfelter 1975; Meggitt 1977; Oliver 1955, 1974; Patterson 1974–75; Rappaport 1968; Vayda 1960; Watson 1971; T. Williams 1858; Zegwaard 1959.

Exchanging: Alkire 1977; Brown 1910; Cooper 1971; Davenport 1962; Dutton 1978; Feil 1980; Firth 1959; Fortune 1932; Groves 1972; Handy and Handy 1972; Harding 1967; Kaeppler 1978; Lessa 1950, 1966; Lingenfelter 1975; Malinowski 1922; Mead 1930a, 1938; Meggitt 1974; Oliver 1955, 1973; Pospisil 1963a; Powell 1960, 1965; Ross 1978; Sahlins 1962, 1972; Salisbury 1970; Schwartz 1963; Strathern 1969, 1971; Thomson 1908; Uberoi 1962; Wilkes 1845; T. Williams 1858.

CHAPTER FOUR

Social Relations

THIS chapter will be devoted to a summary of the social relations of the Pacific Islanders during the early periods of Western contact. We shall be looking at the same Islanders who were doing the things already described (residing, traveling by water, gardening, fighting, trading, marrying, dying, and so forth), but this time our focus will be on the social relationships involved in those activities rather than on the activities themselves. Needless to say, no two Island people conceptualized those multifarious relationships in exactly the same ways; nevertheless they do fall into a number of types few enough to permit summarizing.

Most surveys of this kind begin with some discussion of that allegedly universal type of social unit, the family. Something like what most English-speakers conceive to be a family was indeed to be found in all Island societies, but in so many variants that they can be best understood in context of the many other institutions that served to shape them. One of the most determinative and widespread types of those institutions was that based on concepts regarding descent.

DESCENT UNITS

Descent, as herein employed, refers to the concept whereby a person is identified as being related to an ancestor or ancestress through his (or her) parent, that parent's parent, and so on in ascending generations. Based on this concept, a descent unit is a social unit, either a group of interacting persons or a named category of persons (and in some cases, spirits) formed exclusively or mainly through descent. In cases where the descent is traced unilineally and through females exclusively it is called matrilineal, or if through males patrilineal. And in those societies where descent could be traced both through males and females it will be called ambilineal (from Latin, *ambi-*, 'both'); that is, from either mother or father, and either mother's mother or father, and so on. Let us begin with a résumé of matrilineal descent units.

Matrilineal Descent Units

Societies containing matrilineal descent units were located throughout the Marshall and Caroline islands, in New Britain, New Ireland, the northern Solomons, Guadalcanal, parts of the New Hebrides, the Massim area (east of New Guinea), and along some stretches of the New Guinea coasts. Because of their similarity in descent reckoning, it is justifiable to class them together, but their wide differences in other aspects of descent-unit organization, etc., can be suggested with some examples, beginning with those of the Nagovisi.

The 2,000 or so Papuan-speaking Nagovisi occupied a foothill area of southwestern Bougainville, where they grew taro, raised pigs, engaged in some fishing and hunting, and were domiciled in clusters of two- to five-household hamlets. Crosscutting this residential arrangement were numerous small, named matrilineages, which were parts of matriclans, which were in turn parts of matrimoieties (from French moiété, 'half').

Each matrilineage consisted of persons who traced matrilineal descent from a common ancestress, usually about four generations above the oldest living member. All Nagovisi land was owned corporately, but provisionally, by one or another of its matrilineages, whose female members (and their husbands and unmarried sons) resided and gardened there. (Upon his marriage a man moved to his wife's hamlet and lost most of his rights in his own matrilineage land.)

In turn, contiguous matrilineages were combined into separately named matriclans, which had a number of functions. First, all of the land owned by members of a lineage was in fact only provisionally theirs; reversionary, or residual, rights in it were held by the whole clan of which the lineage was a part. That is, when all members of a lineage died, their land reverted to the clan as a whole, whose leaders allocated it to another lineage of the clan. (In other words, a male member of a lineage could not pass on his rights in its land to his offspring, who were, of course, members of their mother's lineage and not his.) Second, each clan owned residually a hoard of shell-bead heirlooms used for ritual and other purposes. And third, each clan was a separate "church," having owned the shrines and the religious rites that were performed on behalf of its members (e.g., at birth, marriage, death).

A particularly noteworthy feature of Nagovisi clans was the ranking of their respective lineages. Within each clan the lineage tracing its descent from the eldest daughter of the clan's legendary common ancestress was labeled Firstborn, and its members were owed deference from members of the junior lineages of the clan.

In addition, every Nagovisi clan was perceived to be a division of one or the other of the society's two matrimoieties, the Hornbills or the Eagles. Hornbills were expected to refrain from touching or eating birds of that species (i.e., their totems) under pain of sickness, as were Eagles with their avian counterparts. Moreover, each moiety was associated with a separate female spirit, whose assistance was solicited on some ritual occasions. How those totems and tutelar spirits came to be linked with their adherents was not explained: they were not thought of as ancestresses or as "motherly"; in fact, the lands owned by their respective clans were scattered, intermixed, throughout the Nagovisi area, and Eagles fought against Eagles as regularly as against Hornbills. Except for their common totemic and spirit–tutelary connections the only thing shared by all members of either moiety was their exogamy: Eagles should not marry Eagles nor Hornbills Hornbills (from which derived the rule that their clans and matrilineages were also exogamous).

Let us now take a look at the internal structure of Nagovisi descent units. With some exceptions, the head of each lineage was its eldest non-senile female member, called its Firstborn; it was she who had final say over distribution of use-rights in the lineage's (provisionally held) land, over marriage of young members, and over use of the lineage's holdings in clan heirlooms. (Exception to the above occurred in some lineages, where the Firstborn's authority was superceded by that of a junior but richer and more assertive woman, called a *momiako*.) Beyond this lineage level there was, however, no higher authority in Nagovisi's descent-unit system of organization. Firstborn (or *momiako*) heads of Firstborn lineages may have been more influential than other members of a clan in conducting clan-linked ritual and in reassigning lands vacated by an expired lineage, but that was all. And among a moiety's several clans, none of them exercised authority over the rest.

But where did Nagovisi men fit into this system of female-regulated lineages and clans? As noted above, most men moved to their wife's hamlet upon marriage; even one who did not do so was expected to devote most of his efforts to the material well-being of his wife and her lineage-mates, who of course included his own children. (In contrast to most Island marital exchanges, wherein the husband's relatives paid bride-price to relatives of the bride, in Nagovisi the latter paid dowry to the former, evidently to compensate them for their nearly total loss of the man's services.) But it should not be concluded from this that the husband remained an underprivileged and stigmatized outsider in his wife's hamlet. On the contrary, husbands were everywhere heads of their respective households and leaders of their hamlets in matters not directly concerned with descent-unit ritual and the disposition of descent-unit heirlooms and land, matters that included warfare and a kind of competitive feast-giving, renown-seeking activity similar to that of their neigh-

Figure 4.1. Truk, wooden canoe prow

bors, the Siuai, described earlier. In fact, the areas over which some men came to exert political influence may have been larger than any (female) Firstborn's area of influence over descent-unit matters, but the activities of the two spheres seem to have been mutually reinforcing rather than divisive.

We turn next to the society occupying the large complex of Caroline islands called Truk. The 10,000–12,000 members of this society subsisted on breadfruit, taro, sweet potatoes, coconuts, and fish. They resided in widely scattered two- and three-household hamlets.

All of Truk's land was subdivided into estates, each of which was identified, corporately, by full or residual title, with sets of persons interrelated through close ties of matrilineal descent (i.e., by traceable descent from a common ancestress no more than a few generations back). Each such matrilineage was distinctively labeled, and its members were united by sentiments of mutual cooperation and obligation, but not, it seems, by alleged kinship with any species of animal or plant (i.e., Trukese lineages seem not to have been totemic). Each matrilineage had its own building (where males assembled to socialize, to nap, and to store their canoes) and large earth ovens where males prepared food for formal presentation to the district chief (discussed later on) and to any lineages from which they happened to lease land. In addition, some persons resided on their own lineage land; these were in most cases a set of sisters (and their parents, if alive) together with their (nonmember) husbands, their daughters, and their unmarried sons. In other words, marital residence was, as in Nagovisi, uxorilocal; unlike Nagovisi men, however, a Trukese man retained strong ties with his own lineage after marriage, including the sharing of its resources and obligations as well as in its governance. Because of this circumstance, most men married women who resided nearby, the easier to fulfill their responsibilities both as husbands and as brothers.

Unlike those of Nagovisi, the men of Truk had strong voices in the governance of their own lineages. In fact, final authority over use of a lineage's resources and over much of the behavior of lineage members was shared by its Oldest Brother (the eldest male of the eldest generation) and his counterpart, Oldest Sister.

All of Truk's lineages were subdivisions of one or another of the society's forty-two matriclans. The latter averaged about 250 members each but in fact varied widely in size, some containing a single lineage on a single island, others many lineages on many islands (including a few islands outside Truk itself).Except for a single-lineage clan (doubtless one that was dying out), the only things shared in common by all clanmates were a common name, a tradition (though usually undocumentable) of descent from a remote common ancestress, and a proscription on intermarriage. (This proscription was vigorously enforced among lineage-mates, but less so among clanmates not belonging to the same lineage.)

The only ranking that obtained among members of separate lineages of the same clan occurred when a lineage split into two or more independent land-holding units but remained in the same political district. In such situations the eldest of the two lineage's respective Oldest Brothers served as head of both of them in common activities, such as large fish drives and feast preparations. Otherwise (and unlike Nagovisi) the lineages themselves were not ranked.

Like descent units everywhere, Truk's matrilineages underwent change. Some of them died out altogether (i.e., they contained no more child-bearing females); others became so reduced in numbers that they merged with another with which they shared legendary ties of matrilineal descent; and still others proliferated, in numbers and in property, to such an extent that they eventually split. The latter development typically occurred when men came to acquire large amounts of land from their fathers (say, land owned by the latter as sole members of an expiring lineage). By passing on such land to *their* children, the basis was laid for formation of a separate descent line, which might in time become an entirely separate lineage, but a matrilineal one. (Here then is another feature of descent-unit practice in which Truk differed from Nagovisi. In the latter society, it will be recalled, when a lineage's last potential child-bearing female died, ownership of its land passed to another, contiguously located, lineage of its clan.)

Crosscutting Truk's system of descent units and their estates was one of districts, literally "sections of the land," each with its own chief. Truk's districts were founded in either one of two ways: by a man staking out ownership of a previously unpopulated and unowned piece of land, or by one lineage defeating a chiefly one in war. In the case of the pioneer settler, he acquired full title to the land. Later, however, when use of that land (i.e., provisional title to it) passed to his children, and eventually to their lineage, they were required to pay "rent" to the pioneer's own lineage, which thereafter retained residual title to it, and whose senior male became the land's (the new district's) chief. In the case of a district's chiefly lineage being defeated in war, the main lineage of the victors simply assumed the district's chieftainship, with its residual rights in the estates of other lineages located there.

The words district and chief conjure up images of large political units and powerful authority. In fact, Truk's districts were very small, averaging about 100 residents each, and a chief's authority was limited to initiating war (but did not include power to force his subjects to fight), to keeping the peace (again, through persuasion rather than coercion), and to receiving rents (which, however, were eventually returned to the lessee lineages). Nor did he possess any religious functions or special powers. And although he could act with effective authority, as Oldest Brother, over his own lineagemates, he was expected to be "fatherly" (i.e., to act with altruism) toward other residents of his district.

For a third example of matrilineal descent units we go to Busama, a nucleated community of about 600 persons whose dwellings were located on a narrow strip of land along the shores of New Guinea's Huon Gulf. (The Busama shared their Austronesian language with about 6,500 persons living in nearby communities, some friendly, some hostile.) Most Busama households, the community's subsistence units, consisted of a single nuclear family; the heads of the few two-family ones were related either as brothers or as father and married son, or as a man and his sister's married son.

The shoreside residential part of Busama was owned in common by all its residents (by mutual agreement, it seems; there was no community-wide authority to allocate housesites or enforce peaceable coexistence). The gardening land of the village was, however, divided into numerous matrilineage estates. As in Truk, when a Busama man pioneered previously uncleared and unowned land he passed it to his sons, but it then became part of the latters' matrilineage estates. Evidently, unclaimed land was so plentiful that a household had no need to garden on land other than that belonging to the lineages of husband and wife, hence complications regarding provisional and residual rights did not arise.

And, because marital residence was invariably virilocal, a husband did not have to divide his time between two households, as was the case on Truk.

In addition to their estates in land, Busama lineages were exogamous and owned particular rites and ritual offices of a community-wide nature (e.g., for victory in warfare and safety on overseas trading voyages). Also, on every estate was a sacred place (a cave, dense thicket, etc.) in which lived some so-called "spirits of the land"; and although these were not deemed to be relatives of the lineage members owning the estate in a totemic way, they did "permit" lineage members to make use of the land in exchange for occasional offerings. Male lineagemates also tended to occupy contiguous dwellings, in clusters of four or five, and to work together in clearing lineage land (which was then cultivated separately by their respective households). On the other hand, unlike those of Nagovisi and Truk, Busama's lineages were not considered to be segments of clans or other descent units of wider span. Nor did they, as units, play any role in community governance. That governance, such as it was, derived from membership in numerous neighborhood clubs, whose leaders became so because of their wealth and managerial abilities, rather than their seniority in lineages (a situation that resembled that of the Siuai *mumi* institution in some respects).

Thus, Busama lineages were less important parts of the Busama polity than were those of Nagovisi and Truk. Moreover, although membership in them devolved *through* females, the latter played only minor roles in lineage affairs.

Matrilineal descent units were present in dozens of Island societies, but one or more of the three examples of them just sketched contained most of the features found in one or another of the rest.

Their most widely common feature had to do with sex and marriage, namely, a rule that members of the same descent unit ought to refrain from marrying or even having sex with one another. The social sanctions that supported this rule were reinforced in many societies by supernatural penalties as well, but all such sanctions tended to weaken correlative to a unit's span (i.e., to the range of collateral kin included in it). Thus, in societies with three levels of descent-unit segmentation (i.e., lingeage, clan, and moiety), although sex or marriage with a matrilineage mate was so wrong or even sinful as to be virtually unthinkable, sex with a distant moiety mate was regarded as only mildly improper, and even marriage was tolerated in some cases.

The next most widely common feature had to do with land. In nearly every society containing matrilineal descent units they were the principal, in some places the only, social units that owned land. In some societies the full or residual land titles were held at the lowest level of descent-unit segmentation, what is herein labeled the matrilineage level. In other places residual titles were held by higher-level units (e.g., clans), with matrilineages holding only provisional titles to the lands their members resided on and gardened.

In many such societies their matrilineal descent units owned other goods as well, including buildings, heirlooms, and religious rites and offices, which leads us to the important religious aspect of such units.

Among Islanders, unversed as they were in biological genetics, the concept of descent was inherently a religious idea: *something* passed from parent to child that served to unite them in a distinctive and exclusive way, and that something was mystical. (Menstrual blood or semen, or both, were in many societies believed to be vehicles of transmission, but not all menstrual blood and semen were intrinsically spiritual.) Moreover, according to such doctrines, that mystical entity, which had originated with a descent unit's common ancestor or ancestress, had in many cases been transmitted to some prototypical animal or plant as well, thereby linking its descendant species with their human collaterals into what anthropologists call a totemic kind of mystical relationship.

Mystical relationships of many kinds abound in Island cosmologies. The kind now being described, based on common descent, included several specific beliefs and practices. One was that all the members of a common-descent unit were related to one another as quasi siblings or as quasi parent and child, hence ought to behave toward one another amicably, cooperatively, and sexually abstentious. (In many Island languages the eating of one's totem was termed "incest.") Also widespread was the belief that matters having to do with an individual's biological life, especially his or her birth, health, and death, were the concern mainly of his or her descent-unit mates. Hence most of the rites pertaining to such situations were owned (literally) and performed by descent-unit mates. (In Nagovisi, for example, even though a husband resided and associated socially with his wife's lineage, upon death his body was returned to his own lineage-mates to conduct his funeral.) But perhaps the most telling evidence of belief in the mystical unity of descent-unit mates was the widely held belief, and attendant practices, that harm suffered by one member affected all of them, including the proposition that to kill one of a killer's descent-unit mates was as satisfactory as killing the killer himself.

In addition to (or perhaps in extension of) the genealogical aspect of descent-unit relationships, the descent units of many Island societies were associated with other, nonancestral, types of spirits as well (e.g., with major "universal" deities, with genies of their lands, and so forth), to most of which a unit's "priest" addressed petitions and made offerings on behalf of the unit's membership. In fact, in some societies such practices constituted the largest-scale form of public religious activity.

All the above regarding religion applies to Island descent units in general, including matrilineal ones. In fact, in several societies religion was the most salient aspect of their matrilineal descent units, much more so than was their political aspect, to which we now turn.

In most Island societies political activities (e.g., large-scale fighting between communities, intracommunity order keeping, competitive feast giving) were engaged in collectively mainly by males and by those who resided contiguously. In cases where most of the male members of any descent unit resided in the same community, they may have participated, as a unit, in the community's warfare, etc., but, as we shall see, that occurred more often in patrilineally oriented societies than in matrilineal ones. The practice of uxorilocal residence that prevailed in many of the latter served to disperse the male members of its descent units, and even in those where virilocality prevailed, as in Busama, the numbers of descent-unit mates residing close to one another were too small, in comparison with other community groupings, to constitute war-making or other political-action groups.

Next to be considered is the internal social structure of descent units in general and of matrilineal descent units in particular. This is a topic easily disposed of, because the patterns were nearly everywhere the same; namely, among members of most descent units the person(s) who ranked highest received most deference and made the crucial decisions regarding unit matters, such as use and disposal of land and other unit property, marriage of members, religious ritual, and so forth. And the highest ranks in most descent units were held by the oldest members of their senior generations. One exception to this widespread principle had to do with mental fitness: in many places when the most senior member of a descent unit became senile he (or she) gave place to someone younger, especially if the unit played an important political role. Another exception had to do with sex: it was only in matrilineal descent units (and in not all of them) that women ranked higher than their "brothers" of similar seniority.

From ranking within autonomous descent units or descent-unit segments we turn to ranking between the segments of units of wider span. In some societies no such ranking prevailed, but in many more of them it did, and was in most cases based on one or another of three rationales. The first and most common was seniority: the segment that was nearest, in birth order and generation, to the encompassing units' founding ancestor(ress) ranked highest, and so on down the genealogical pyramid. A second rationale for ranking, especially in areas where land was scarce (as, for example, on atoll islets) was priority of settlement; typically, the first segment of a descent unit to have occupied an area ranked higher than subsequent segments, regardless of seniority (even if such were known). Third, in places where one descent unit had defeated, and either replaced or submerged, another in war the victors tended to be ranked higher than the rest regardless of their previous relationships.

Patrilineal Descent Units

Societies in which all descent units were patrilineal were located in New Guinea (where they greatly outnumbered all others), in the southeastern Solomons, the central and southern New Hebrides, New Caledonia, the Loyalty Islands, Fiji, and in at least one Polynesian island, Tikopia. Continuing the procedure followed in surveying matrilineal descent units, I shall describe the patrilineal ones of three societies in some detail and use them as bases for generalizing about all the others. I begin with the Mae Enga.

The 36,000–37,000 Mae Enga occupied about 300 square miles of the New Guinea Highlands between altitudes of 4,500 to 7,500 feet. Their staple crop was sweet potatoes, supplemented by other root crops and leafy vegetables. They raised pigs and did a little hunting and collecting. Like many other Highlanders, their men engaged frequently in large-scale, prestige-building, ally-seeking gift-exchange. Their descent-unit system contained five levels of segmentation (as compared with Nagovisi's three, Truk's two, and Busama's one); in descending order of span these were (following the labels given them by their ethnographer, Mervyn Meggitt) phratries (from Greek, 'brother'), clans, subclans, lineages, and sub-lineages. The fourteen phratries contained an average of eight clans each, the clans an average of four subclans each, subclans an average of two lineages each, and lineages contained the agnatic (i.e., related through male descent) cores of an average of seven families. According to the Mae Engas' beliefs, their original ancestors were (male) Sun and (female) Moon; these two begot numerous Sky People, some of whom descended to earth and begot humans, who became the founders of phratries (in the local language, "a great line of men"). Then, the human male phratry-founders begot sons, who founded clans, and so on. In addition, some Sky People brought fertility stones to earth, and these, along with certain pools of water, became the foci of (clan) rituals carried out to propitiate ghosts and ensure (clan) welfare. Of all the above levels of segmentation, that of the clan was most important, inasmuch as each of them constituted the nucleus of a distinct community.

The average community contained about 350 persons residing in a sharply boundaried territory of about one square mile in area. Because clans were exogamous (phratries were not) and marital residence mostly virilocal, the majority of residents in any community consisted of the adult male members of the owning clan along with their wives (mostly from other communities) and unmarried children. In addition, most communities also contained several outsiders, such as mother-related kinfolk of the local clan members, along with kinfolk of the latters' wives. Uncontested use-rights over portions of the clan's territory were held by individual adult male clan members, who passed those rights to their sons, but residual rights over all the territory were retained by the clan as a whole. An adult clan member could permit an outsider (say, a relative of his mother or of his wife) to reside and garden on his portion of clan territory temporarily, but the consent of his clanmates was required to give permanence to the arrangement. During his lifetime the outsider remained a kind of second-class citizen, but his offspring usually became accepted as full-fledged community members, provided they behaved as such and were no longer loyal to their father's natal clan. And eventually, when memory of their origins faded, their descendants were considered to be full members of the local clan.

In the case of most outsiders, their reason for moving out of their own clan communities was shortage of land. And the main reason for their acceptance by their hosts was the latters' desire for more fighters to protect their boundaries from neighboring land-hungry clans. In other words, although the Mae Enga held steadfastly to the dogma that all male members of a clan were "a line of men descended from one penis," they occasionally bent that dogma for practical reasons.

In addition to fighting as a unit in intercommunity wars, the members of each clan acted collectively, for example, to pay war indemnities, to engage in large-scale intercommunity competitive gift giving, and to conduct rites to propitiate their clan's ancestral ghosts.

The territories of clans making up a phratry were usually contiguous, but the only activities that such clans engaged in collectively, and those only occasionally, were religious rites and fights against common enemies.

The activities engaged in by members of any segment of a clan differed according to level (e.g., subclanmates sponsored each others' mortuary feasts and other life-crisis rites, and lineagemates cooperated in some subsistence activities and in the financing of each others' bride-price payments). The sublineage (consisting of a married male and his unmarried offspring) was the nucleus of each household and the holder of use-rights in specific plots of land. Speaking of which, the sequence in which land rights passed from one level to another ideally followed the order of segmentation, but of course in reverse, with the phratry being the ultimate residuary. In practice, however, because the fraternal clans of a phratry were in most instances unable to defend one another's territory against enemy attack, each clan was largely autonomous and the de facto residual owner of its members' lands.

Just as the patterns of Mae Enga land tenure and collective activities corresponded to the levels of descent-unit segmentation, so did that of leadership. For example, when a young man was deemed ready for marriage his father arranged most of the preliminaries with the father of the bride, but final arrangements were made by the leaders of the couple's respective lineages. Or, when a man died it was the right and duty of the

leader of his subclan, and not of his lineage, to supervise funeral arrangements (although in some cases the leader of lineage and subclan were the
same man). Again, when some individual set in motion a train of events
leading to interclan hostilities it was the leader of his whole clan, and
ipso facto community, who directed the ensuing war. Who those leaders
were, however, is another question.

Unlike most of the (matrilineal) descent-unit systems so far considered, seniority played little part in succession to leadership in Mae Enga
descent units higher than the family (i.e., sub-lineage) level. Instead,
leadership was achieved, and by success in a number of ways (e.g., by
exercising skill as manager and arbitrator, by winning local supporters
through generosity, and by acquiring prestige and foreign allies through
the kind of gift-exchanging described earlier). In much of this the
aspiring leader had to depend upon support from his close kinsmen and
affines, but the process of becoming a leader (especially of subclans and
clans) required single-minded commitment, boundless energy, political
shrewdness, and diplomatic finesse. And even after such leadership had
been attained, it could be maintained only by continuation of the same
kinds of behavior, which no individual seems to have been able to sustain
for more than a decade or so.

Similarly, just as individuals were not ranked within their descent units
by seniority or other forms of ascription, so whole units were not ranked
vis-à-vis each other, as was the case in Nagovisi.

For a second example of patrilineal descent units, we turn to New
Caledonia, at the southern end of Melanesia. This island, 160 miles long
and 30 miles wide, had a population of 30,000–40,000 at the time Europeans first saw it, in 1774. The Island's twenty-eight Austronesian languages shared enough grammatical features to give them a measure of
unity in comparison with Austronesian languages elsewhere, a homogeneity that extended to other aspects of the island's cultures as well. The
main food crops were taro and yams; chickens were domesticated, but
not pigs; fishing was actively engaged in, but hunting far less so. Except
for its dry southwestern grasslands, the island was extensively though
thinly populated. Communities were widely dispersed and most of them
quite small, having been on the average a compact cluster of five to ten
households separated from all other communities by wide stretches of
garden lands and forests. In its smallest and simplest variant, a community consisted physically of a long rectangular plaza flanked by beehive-
shaped family dwellings and terminated by a larger clan house, where
men spent much of their nonworking time; it was closed to women
except on occasion and served as the clan's "church" (i.e., for seances
with and offerings to its ancestors and other tutelar spirits). Most of a
community's public life (festivals, dances, etc.) took place in the plaza;
the spaces behind the houses were reserved mainly for women and for

visiting members of the wives' own clans (or, in native terms, for "mothers' brothers").

So far I have referred, loosely, to New Caledonia's "clans." I must now be more precise. The task is complicated by the absence in most of the printed sources of distinctions among types and levels of clan segmentation, but all sources agree that such clans were exogamous, totemic, and (ideally) patrilineal.

The smallest institutionalized clan segment, the lineage, consisted of a locally domiciled set of adult men (and their offspring) who considered themselves to be descended through males from a common male ancestor usually no more than about three generations back. The married sisters of those men were also counted as members of the lineage but resided in their husbands' communities, which were usually elsewhere. Some of the units referred to in the literature as clans may have consisted of single lineages, but most clans seem to have contained two or more lineages, whose interconnections, however, were not all of the same kind.

One kind was exemplified in communities containing two or more lineages claiming common (patrilineal) descent. In all such cases, one of the lineages (the one that was senior in terms of the birth-order of its eponymous ancestor, or the one whose ancestor had first occupied the place) was superior in rank to the others. In another quite common variant of single-clan, multi-lineage communities, one (or more) of the lineages seems to have been, originally, a segment of another clan, a segment that had become integrated into the current clanlike unit in consequence of defeat by the local segment or, at its own seeking, because of its migration from elsewhere. (Like most Island peoples, the New Caledonians were adept in inventing myths and genealogies to incorporate outsiders into their, ideally, ascriptively exclusive social units.) In other cases, single clans were composed of lineages localized in several different places, some of them many miles apart. One circumstance that contributed to this arrangement was the scantiness of the population relative to the Island's extensive arable land. Another was its topography, which imposed few obstructions to movement. And a third was the tendency, evidently quite common, for lineagemates, and especially brothers, to solve their conflicts with one another by one of them moving away. In any case, and whatever the causes, the maps constructed by ethnographers picture single clans dispersed over wide areas, even across language boundaries, their lineages interspersed and their respective legendary migration routes intricately crisscrossed.

As mentioned earlier, in cases where two or more lineages of the same clan were domiciled in the same or in closely neighboring communities, one was held to be senior to the others, but the implications of such seniority were confined largely to the senior lineage's headman, who was ex officio headman of all other local lineages of the clan. The nature of that

Figure 4.2. New Caledonia: *a,* wood carving; *b,* mask

office can be made clearer by listing some other clan-associated offices. One such was "master of the soil," whose exclusive right and duty it was to communicate with the ancestral and other spirits that exercised control over the lineage's (or clan's) lands, and hence over the material welfare of the members. This office was reserved for a community's pioneer lineage or clan and was usually held by that unit's oldest male member. In single-clan communities the offices of headman and master of the soil were combined in one man, but in more complex communities that was often not the case. Another office was clan priest, whose right and duty it was to communicate with other of the clan's tutelar spirits. Unlike headmanship and soil-mastership, this office was reserved for one of the clan's junior lineages, and within that unit it usually passed from father to son. Two other offices, which obtained in some clans and in most or all larger multi-clan communities, were war leader and war priest.

The clan headman had a leading voice in deciding, say, when to go to war or when to communicate with spirits on behalf of the whole clan, but he himself did not engage in fighting or in petitioning (except when he was soil-master as well). And even though he had an influential voice in decisions respecting his clan, his was not the only voice; most such matters were decided in council with other clan officials. In fact, his principal rights and duties were to announce those decisions, to initiate clan activities ceremoniously, and to glorify the clan's past (in the form of perorations concerning the clan's divine origins, its vicissitudinous migrations, its martial victories, and the miraculous and heroic acts of its ancestors). The ability to perform these actions required long and arduous training. The prime candidate for the office was the current headman's oldest son, but if he proved incapable of performing this exacting part of the office, the clan elders chose another candidate, including even in some cases a member of a lineage recently incorporated into the clan.

As previously mentioned, New Caledonia's clans were exogamous. And although it was permissible for a person to marry anyone of any clan but his own there was a decided preference for a man to marry a member of his mother's clan (a "mother's brother's daughter"). A person's relationship with his mother's lineage, including especially his mother's own brother, was colored, typically, by affection and mutual support.

After a series of marriages between particular pairs of clans, the practice developed into a rule. And because alliance based on marriage called forth amicable relationships generally, each clan came in time to be linked with several others in durable marital-based pacts of peace and exchange. Moreover, in some parts of the island the connections of this kind developed into extensive groupings of the clans into large and named units, whereby members of one unit married into the other one, a system reminiscent of Nagovisi moieties, though not canonized in terms of common descent.

Another way in which some clans were interrelated was by common allegiance to the headman of one of them. These chiefdoms varied in size and coherence from single multi-clan communities to some containing numerous communities (and clans), including a few whose territories were not all contiguous or whose members did not all speak the same language. Several kinds of situations served to create these unities: warfare (either as a consequence of victory or defeat, or by voluntary attachment for purpose of protection); matrimonial alliance; desire for barter, and so forth; and the ambitions of individuals for the kinds of privileges, etc., that chieftainship of this type permitted. However, such chiefdoms did not hold together for more than a few generations and although succession to leadership in them ideally passed from father to son, other factors intervened to make particular chiefly dynasties short-lived.

For the third example we turn to Tikopia, the only society of Polynesian-speakers whose descent units were unequivocally patrilineal.

Tikopia, the easternmost outlier of the Solomon chain, consists of the mountainous rim of a crater lake and contains about six square miles of land. In 1928, when it was first studied, its population of about 1,300 was still mainly pagan, and pre-European in most other cultural respects as well. Its people kept neither pigs nor chickens but were well supplied with vegetable foods and fish. Their settlements consisted of fifteen communities, each containing several households, whose dwellings were described in chapter 3. Some communities also contained one or two temples (i.e., the past dwellings of notable ancestors). Each community had its name and its commonly acknowledged boundaries, and its residents often interacted in groups: the women to harvest the reefs, the men to fish together as a fleet, young people to dance together in the evenings, and so forth. And although members of separate communities often assembled for some purpose or other they did so with expressed consciousness of their separate community identities. Tikopia was also divided into two districts (*fasi*, 'sides') separated in part by mountain ridges. Formerly the two districts used to fight one another, and even under the colonial peace the rivalry persisted in the form of mutual wariness and disparagement.

Cutting across both community and district boundaries were descent units, called *paito*, each of which contained an average of thirty to sixty members, who were all of the living descendants in the male line of some genealogically traceable ancestor of a few generations past. Typically, the members of a *paito* consisted of a set of elderly or middle-aged persons, males and females, interrelated by sibling or other close patrilateral ties (e.g., first and second cousins), plus all the sons and daughters of the males of the above, plus the sons and daughters of those sons, etc., etc. Any child of any of the above females would have belonged to the *paito* of its father, which in most but not all cases would have differed from that of its mother, not because of any explicit prohibition against marrying within the *paito*, but because of a general prohibition against marrying a close consanguine, whether patrilateral or matrilateral. (Marriage with a first cousin was strongly and universally disapproved, and with a second cousin frowned upon.) In other words, the Tikopian *paito* conforms to our definition of a lineage (in this case a patrilineage), but one that was not explicitly exogamous.

One rationale for the patrilineality of their lineages was contained in the Tikopian theory of conception. Women were believed to serve only as receptacles for fetuses, whose basic physical material was supplied by semen. In due course a female deity helped to shape the growing fetus, and a soul (*ora, mauri*) was implanted in it from outside, but the resulting child was considered to be mainly the product of its genitor. Moreover, membership in a lineage was strictly limited to individuals believed to have been conceived by a male member; unlike some other Polynesian descent units an individual could not be adopted into it. Moreover, the adult members of a lineage were able to trace their presumed descent to some named, historical rather than legendary, human ancestor through patrilines of actual and name-identified genealogical links. In the case of chiefly lineages, such lines were traced back for ten or so generations, and even beyond that with respect to mythical or supernatural forebears. For most nonchiefly *paito,* however, the eponymous ancestor (the one credited with having founded it as a separate unit) went back no farther than four or so generations.

Each lineage had its own proper name and a number of corporately owned tracts of land; the whole Island was divided into such estates. One or more of each lineage's estates contained house sites, including one or more temples containing the graves of former members. Moreover, the estates of each lineage included some areas planted in tree crops and others given over to gardening. In most cases a lineage's estates were scattered widely over the island, but its male and unmarried female members (marital residence was mostly virilocal) tended to dwell in houses near one another and usually, but not necessarily, on their own estates.

Among any set of siblings the oldest son was accorded most authority and privilege. This principle carried over into lineage organization as well; the titular head of a lineage was usually the most direct descendant from the eponymous ancestor in the line of senior sons. As head he was titular controller over his lineage's estates and sacred canoes and represented its members vis-à-vis their ancestral ghost-guardians and deities. He also exercised some control over other aspects of his lineagemates' behavior, but that was consciously limited by their having been his close consanguines and by the overarching powers held by the chief of whichever clan *(kainanga)* his lineage was a division of, of which more will be said later.

The size of individual lineages varied as a result of uneven demographic events. Some of them became greatly reduced or even died out altogether (i.e., their surviving male members produced no sons), while others increased enough to encourage branching into separate lineages. In some cases the branching resulted from strife among brothers, but most typically it seems to have been a normal concomitant of numerical increase. There was no official enactment to transform a branch into a recognized lineage; it was usually a gradual process. Once established, however, a lineage continued to exist as a separate entity until every member expired, in which event its lands and other properties usually reverted to the lineage from which it had branched.

Every lineage was included in one or another of Tikopia's four *kainanga,* or clans, which derived their names from the senior one of its lineages, whose head was also chief *(Te Ariki)* of the clan. Most lineages owed their inclusion in their respective clans as result of branching from an original lineage, but a few did so as a result of incorporation (i.e., some male immigrant having married a daughter or sister of his local protector, thereby siring children, who for lack of alternative, became members of their mother's lineage and whose own patrilineal descendants eventually became a separate lineage).

Even more than in the case of their constituent lineages, the lands and members of each clan were scattered throughout the island, hence clanmates were often divided by their different community and district loyalties. But their ultimate authority in both secular and religious matters was the chief (the *Ariki*) of their own clan.

Tikopian clans functioned as units in dance contests, dart matches, in some kinds of feasting, in funeral rites for their chiefs, and so forth, but mostly in seasonal religious rites having to do with food supplies and health. With regard to food, each clan was responsible for ensuring, through rites directed to its particular deities, the growth of one or another of the four major food crops: taro, yams, coconuts, or breadfruit. The particular deities *(atua)* revered by each clan included the apotheosized spirits of some of its former members along with some spirits that had never been human.

Usually the office of clan chief devolved upon the oldest son of the reigning office holder, and immediately after the latter's death. If, however, the chief had no male issue or none of adult age, or if some influential clanmates wished to return the office to the main (i.e., senior) line of descent after it had been held for a while in a collateral line, contention could and sometimes did occur. But after a candidate had been ritually installed he usually held office for life, an office that invested him with far-reaching religious and secular authorities.

A chief's secular authority applied most powerfully and directly to members of his own clan but extended over other persons as well, in that he was treated by all Tikopians with great deference. In fact, he had the power to exile any person who aroused his wrath, and exile, which meant setting forth alone in a small canoe, usually meant death.

In household subsistence matters a chief depended mainly upon his own labor and that of his closest relatives; most of the goods he received from clanmates (i.e., on ceremonial occasions) he redistributed at the time or eventually reciprocated. In fact, in terms of material goods (e.g., bearing coconut palms and breadfruit trees, garden produce) there were some nonchiefs who owned as much or more than some chiefs. But in terms of land, the most important form of property, a chief had rights that superceded those of any of his clanmates; the cardinal principle was that all the land held by any member of a clan was at the chief's disposal. In the words of the ethnographer Raymond Firth, "The chief is the head of the clan, its representative with the gods, mediator for his people in regard to the fertility of their crops. Hence his control of supernatural forces in the interests of his people on the one hand should be matched by control of their material resources on the other" (1936:376).

One expression of a chief's overlordship was the voluntary "gifts" of food (tribute) made to him by his clanmates from time to time. A second was his right to levy food and services from clan members for religious ceremonies and other distributions sponsored by him. And a third, more direct, expression was a chief's intervention in the quarrels between clanmates over contested estates; if they persisted in their contentions against his advice he could and sometimes did himself assume direct ownership of the estates.

Just as a chief's secular authority was enforced (and sometimes mitigated) by officials known as *maru,* he was assisted in his priestly duties by his clan's several elders *(pure),* who were heads of the clan's other senior lineages.

Although inheritance and succession were mainly patrifilial and a Tikopian owed his primary loyalty to his own lineagemates, including the ghosts of its dead members, he (or she) maintained very close ties with the lineage of his mother as well, especially with his *tuatina,* the brothers of his mother. To the *tuatina* and all other members of his mother's lineage he (or she) was their *tama tapu,* their "sacred child."

A lineage's concern with their "sacred child" (i.e., every child of every one of its female members) began before its birth and continued after its death. If a fetus happened to be positioned incorrectly in the womb, some of its mother's lineagemates corrected it by manipulation, and thereafter one or more representatives of that lineage played an active role at every critical point in the life of the "sacred child."

Finally, something more should be said about the comprehensively hierarchical aspect of Tikopian kin relations, a factor common to all Polynesian societies and one that served to distinguish them, as a whole, from many societies in Melanesia.

In Tikopia the head of a lineage was usually the oldest son of a line of oldest sons leading back to its founder. A corresponding arrangement prevailed among the several lineages making up a clan. Moreover, it was the ideal (though not always the practice) for clan chieftainship to remain within that senior lineage. Tikopia's four clans were also interrelated hierarchically, but not in a thoroughgoing genealogical way. Although the chieftainship of the one called *Kafika* had some rights (and duties) superior to those of the other three, these had to do mainly with religious worship and were accounted for only partly in terms of seniority. On the other hand, although the chief of the *Kafika* clan outranked the chiefs of the other three, that did not make all members of his clan superior to all members of the other three. Instead, each clan's lineages were separated into two social classes: chiefly and commoner. Differences between the two classes were based on seniority and had mainly to do with authority.

Both chiefly and commoner lineages owned estates, and their members often intermarried, but as Firth wrote, "A person of chiefly family, particularly if closely related to the chief himself, is more apt to give than to receive orders" (1936:358). As we shall see, this is far narrower than the gulfs that separated similarly based social strata in some other Polynesian societies.

Summarizing, a rough comparison of patrilineal with matrilineal descent units suggests that they were similar with respect to their importance in owning land and other durable goods and in public religious practices. Some noteworthy differences between the two types did, however, prevail. For example, actual membership in a matrilineal descent unit usually conformed more closely to the descent principle, and matrilineal units tended to be more consistently exogamous, the result, perhaps, of the difficulty of denying or inventing matrifilial ties. On the other hand, patrilineal descent units tended to be much more political (specifically, governmental) than matrilineal ones, due undoubtedly to the actual preponderance of virilocal residence even in matrilineal societies and to the predominance of males in political activities everywhere.

Societies with Two Unilineal Descent Systems

The relatively few societies of this type were represented in Melanesia (New Guinea, Wogeo Island, the Small Islands off the northeast coast of Malekula, northern Ambrym, southern Raga), in Micronesia (Yap), and in Polynesia (Pukapuka, Ontong Java). Among those in Melanesia the best described is Ngaing.

The 800–900 Ngaing people lived inland from New Guinea's Rai Coast in a rainforest region of sharp mountain ridges, deep gorges, and swift rivers. They resided in some twenty well-defined communities, each of which was fairly autonomous politically but interconnected with the others by ties of kinship and trade. Each community consisted of a number (how many is not reported) of named and exogamous patriclans, which were divided into a number of shallow (three to five generations deep) unnamed patrilineages. Atypically, members of a clan did not acknowledge a putative common ancestor.

In addition to its exogamy, the Ngaing patriclan constituted a unit in four important respects. First, in consequence of virilocal residence its male and unmarried female members lived in close proximity to one another as a physically distinct neighborhood. Second, it was the society's basic landowning corporation, as well as the exclusive proprietor of certain kinds of ritual goods (e.g., a whole or part of a cult-house), certain major cult artifacts (e.g., a slit-gong and its distinctive gong beats, gourd trumpets and their distinctive melodies, a sacred water pool), and

Figure 4.3. Yapese
sleeping house

distinctive ceremonies performed for invoking and honoring deceased members (whose good will and assistance were required for the physical and material welfare of living members of their clan). Leadership in a clan had to be achieved, by proven skill in warfare, or gardening, or management of exchanging, or, most important, by mastery of sacred knowledge and ritual. Even so, such leaders had no commanding judiciary authority over fellow clansmen and, despite their monopoly of clan leadership status, little more than persuasive influence outside their own clans.

Each Ngaing was also a member of a named, exogamous, totemic matrilineage of three to five generations in depth. As residence was virilocal, the members of a matrilineage were scattered among several communities, and in some cases lived far apart. Besides identification with their totemic animals and plants, matrilineagemates owned nothing in common and (not surprisingly, in view of their wide scatter) engaged in no activities collectively. On the other hand, the sentiments of kinship and mutuality fostered by co-membership in a matrilineage provided a person with cooperative assistance at home and protection abroad.

The Yap islands of Micronesia are geographically in the Caroline chain but they, along with the Palau islands, seem to have been settled several centuries before the other Caroline islands. And although the people of Yap shared some features of social organization and fairly frequent social interaction with other Caroline islanders, their social institutions contained many traits that set them apart. For example, the society contained two kinds of descent units, one matrilineal and the other patrilineal.

Yap's matriclans *(genung)* were individually named, exogamous, and totemic; except in the case of two of them they possessed no exclusive rights to particular tracts of land, although some of their origin myths did refer to particular places. And although the members of each clan referred to themselves as "one branching tree of people," they (unlike clanmates in many other Island societies) used kinship terms (and correspondingly appropriate modes of behavior) only for those clanmates to whom genealogical connections could be actually traced. With regard to the latter (i.e., the members of a *matrilineage*), the norms called for mutual assistance and loyalty, especially on critical occasions, when the relationship was ideally modeled on that between a mother and her child. When some occasion brought members of a matrilineage together, leadership rested in the hands of the one who combined older age and close genealogical connection with the member being honored or supported. Even so, no matrilineage held permanent rights of tenure in any particular tract of land, although parts of matrilineages possessed a kind of short-term residual right in certain patrilineage estates, as will be shown.

A Yap ideal was for each household to have its own estate, which included residence site, garden lands, associated ancestral spirits and names, and certain authorities or entitlements. On the other hand, not all household members possessed identical kinds of titles (i.e., rights and obligations) in their common estate. In the case of a man residing there who had been born there and had inherited his entitlements from his father, he had what were called *tafen* rights (i.e., permanent and almost exclusive use-rights), which he in turn passed on to his sons. A larger share of *tafen* rights, including occupancy of the estate's "central foundation" house site, passed to his eldest son, but some shares to all of them. In the case of a daughter, she possessed temporary use-rights in the estate before her marriage, and when she left to live on her husband's estate (as women invariably did) she was usually permitted to resume those rights when visiting her natal family or in case of her divorce and return home to live. Also, if there were no sons for a father's rights to pass to, a daughter received the right to transmit *tafen* rights to her children, a circumstance that added considerably to a woman's value as a wife (i.e., her son's thereby received permanent use-rights in two estates).

A woman's stake in her husband's estate was acknowledged by the practice of entitling certain of her matrilineal descendants to serve as trustees of that estate (a set of rights called *mafen,* which may be translated as "a feeling for ownership" and paraphrased as temporary residual rights). Such rights were temporary inasmuch as they were exercisable for only three generations succeeding the woman whose services, as a wife, had instituted them. Because a new matriline was established with every new wife, there were at any one time three different matrilines holding *mafen* rights in each (household) estate. *Mafen* rights tended to diminish with time, but in the case of the most recently instituted matriline of trustees, its eldest member played a very active role in the affairs of an estate, including the right to evict children should they neglect either their father or the land.

When a man had two or more married sons, the younger ones and their wives and children were accommodated by assigning them separate house sites and garden lands, or in some cases by acquiring new lands for them, which eventually became new estates.

There were, thus, in Yap society numerous patrilineages consisting of persons tracing patrilineal descent from a common ancestor three or four generations back. Such a unit was in fact exogamous, but only in the sense that its members were all consanguines, and marriage was prohibited between persons believed to be consanguines. Ideally, patrilineage-mates were expected to be mutually supportive and cooperative. Also, if a man died without issue his *tafen* rights passed to a patrilineagemate (say, to a brother's eldest son). On the other hand, the several separate estates of a set of patrilineagemates did not constitute a single patrilineage heritage, a unified bundle of *tafen* rights.

The thousand and more estates on Yap were grouped into separate *binaw,* which seem to conform to the unit we label community. At the time of their study (1967–1969) there were ninety-one of these actually inhabited, but evidence points to there having been twice as many in the past. With the exception of several low-caste ones (discussed later), the territories of most *binaw* had at least one coastal boundary, with their residential areas near the shore and their contiguous garden areas just inland. Today some of them contain only a few households; formerly some of them may have contained a hundred and more. All the land in every community may at one time have been identified with one or another of its several estates, but some of it was set aside for public use— for paths, dance grounds, official battle grounds, and for three types of buildings: community-wide houses (used mainly by older men), menstrual houses, and clubhouses for young men (in which resided a "hostess," usually a captured woman, who served the young men's sexual needs).

Most of Yap's communities were divided into neighborhoods, which were subdivided into sub-neighborhoods, which were in turn subdivided into patrilineage estates or small "associations" of such estates (including one or more that had been given to an outsider in return for service rendered to its former owner). Estates were ranked within each association and sub-neighborhood, ranking having been based on seniority (among interrelated patrilineages), on donorship (a donor patrilineage ranked higher than its donee), and, it seems, on priority of settlement or victory in warfare. That is to say, one of the entitlements (the "authorities") belonging to one of the estates was the right and duty to be headman of an association or sub-neighborhood.

The same kind of ranking mechanisms prevailed at the level of a community's neighborhoods and of a community as a whole and, as we shall see, at even higher levels of the society's political structure as well. Membership alone in a high-ranking estate conferred some advantage over all members of lower-ranking ones, but mainly in terms of prestige (e.g., of ceremonial deference and respect). In terms of power (of command over persons, objects, and services), that rested solely or mainly in the hands of the individual who headed the household occupying the "central foundation" of the sub-neighborhood's (or neighborhood's, or community's) highest ranking estate, the individual who was the *pilung*, the "voice" of the "authorities" vested in that estate.

However, there was not only one such highest-ranking estate (and hence "voice") in a community, but three, each of whose voices spoke for the estates endowed with such powers. The incumbent of the entitlement possessing general authority over most community-wide affairs (ceremonial, religious, economic, diplomatic, etc.) was the "voice of the community." Although the initiator and the leader in many community affairs, he was guided by a council made up of representatives of the community's other high-ranking estates. The second community official was the "voice of young men," whose estate's entitlement it was to represent the young men in the council and to supervise their collective activities (in carrying out work projects, etc.). It was also his job to look after the community's shell valuables and to represent his community in its dealings with other communities. And third was the community's "ancient voice," whose role was not to initiate or supervise but to sit and listen and act as advisor to the council and community chief. In addition to the above there were in most communities other kinds of officials: a head priest, a leader of net fishing (and a magician of net fishing), a leader of communal gardening (and a gardening magician), a war leader (and a war magician), etc., all of which statuses were entitlements of their incumbents' estates. In the case of the larger communities, the offices of community chief and voice of young men were replicated at the neighborhood and sub-neighborhood levels, as were some of the other functional offices as well.

In addition to the above there were in many communities functional offices of other kinds, but enough has been said to demonstrate that the principal political unit of Yap society, the community, was highly, minutely, and comprehensively organized and was guided and administered by a veritable phalanx of officers whose jobs were explicitly differentiated and for the most part the fixed prerogatives of the incumbents' estates. (It was as if the presidency of the United States were an entitlement of the family owning an estate in, say, Hyannisport!) As was noted earlier, the ideal succession order to estate headship (and thus in many cases to chieftainship, etc.) of a whole community was from father to oldest son, but that ideal was occasionally bent in favor of a better qualified younger brother or nephew. And although specific community offices were, ideally, allocated to specific estates, there were enough ambiguities in that allocation to invite competition for them. And competition there was—in the form of political maneuvering, assassinations, and interneighborhood feuds. As the ethnographers tell us, the quest for political power, within individual communities and on the wider stage, was a pastime of many men, and success even at the community level often depended upon having allies outside.

As for the wider political stage just referred to, Yap society was so pervasively hierarchic and opportunities for raising one's status so numerous (and ambitions for doing this so widespread and compelling) that warfare and political maneuvering were a dominant part of men's life. However, no one man or social unit had within memory succeeded in attaining a monopoly of power or prestige. For some time in the past the quest had evolved into a rivalry between two major alliances split between the society's three most powerful chiefs. When the forces of one of the chiefs seemed to be winning over those of another, the third chief joined forces with the latter to adjust the balance, thereby carrying out a political philosophy that likened the three paramount chieftainships to the three pedestal stones on which a cooking pot rested over a fire (i.e., "if one stone fell the pot would also fall").

In Polynesia, two societies contained both patri- and matrilineal descent units. On the atoll of Pukapuka its patrilineal units were similar to those of Tikopia, described earlier. And although the only activity engaged in by its matrilineal units was to manage the society's precious taro beds (the atoll has little soil to garden in), such units were by rule exogamous, the only clear-cut case of descent-unit exogamy in Polynesia that I know of.

The second Polynesian society containing both patrilineal and matrilineal descent units was that of the very large atoll of Ontong Java, east of the Solomon chain. What the respective functions of those units were is, however, not clear.

Ngaing, Yap, Pukapuka, and Ontong Java represent societies in which a person belonged to both a patrilineal and a matrilineal descent unit. We next consider societies in which a person could affiliate with descent units of either or both of his parents (but in most cases associated mainly with only one of them).

Ambilineal Descent Units

A few societies of this type were located in and around New Guinea (e.g., the Telefolmin, Garia, Huli, Kunimaipa, and Molina); several more were concentrated in the Solomon islands of Choiseul and Malaita; and one

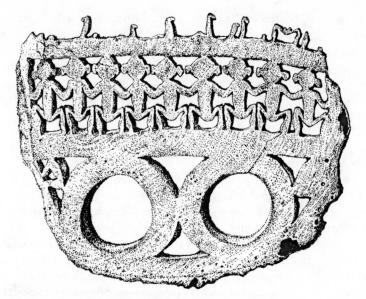

Figure 4.4. Choiseul, Solomon Islands, shell carving

was located in the northern Gilbert Islands. And in Polynesia all except Tikopia, Pukapuka, and Ontong Java were of this type. A résumé will be given of the one on Choiseul, which resembled closely its counterparts on Malaita, but differed considerably from the New Guinea ones. Then, a brief résumé of the Gilbertese one will be given, leaving more space for those of Polynesia, where this type of kinship unit was not only numerically preponderant but religiously and politically dominant as well, and where it occurred in several noteworthy variations.

Choiseul Island is about 80 miles long and 8–20 miles wide. Except for a mountain 3,500 feet high in the center, most of it consists of sharp ridges and plateaus, averaging 1,000 to 2,000 feet in altitude. Outside of gardens, groves, and secondary growth areas in fallow, it is covered by high-canopied rainforest. The pre-European population of 8,000 to 10,000 was distributed fairly evenly over the whole of it, except directly on the coasts, which were vulnerable to raiding by aggressively head-hunting warriors from New Georgia and other islands nearby. Communities were located mostly along the tops of ridges and consisted of small hamlets grouped into neighborhoods. On occasion (e.g., when war threatened or when holding a large feast) the residents of a whole community built and congregated into a more compact and better protected settlement but returned to their hamlets after the threat subsided or the feast ended. A network of paths facilitated intercommunity warfare, but peaceful interaction as well; and although the whole population was divided into different dialect areas, it has been described as having been culturally uniform. The basic food crop everywhere was taro, supplemented by yams and bananas; pigs were raised and used mainly for feasts and other forms of exchange. And even more so than in many other societies of Melanesia, shell money served as an object of exchange and a measure of wealth.

The basic subsistence units were family households; some of these were widely separated but most were clustered into small hamlets. Beyond these the most important entities of Choiseulese society were territorial estates, ambilineal descent categories, and the aforesaid residential communities.

The island was divided into some 150 to 200 major estates, each one named and fairly clearly bounded (e.g., by ridges, streams, rock outcrops, etc.). They varied widely in size; four of those plotted by the ethnographer Harold Scheffler ranged in size from 3.5 to 10.5 square miles and averaged 7.2. Evidently, each major estate contained numerous permanent groves of useful trees (e.g., coconut palms, almond trees), which were used, more or less exclusively, by individuals or groups of estate "owners." Most of the undivided parts of any estate were, however, open to more or less temporary use (for gardening, fishing, collecting) by any and all persons domiciled there. In addition, each estate contained a number of shrines where communication took place between the living residents and spirits, including locally associated deities and ancestral ghosts.

Each major estate was owned by a social category (not an interacting group) composed of all persons generally recognized to be descendants (including adoptees), through either or both parents, of a specific ancestor who in most cases had lived no earlier than six to seven generations back. In his sample of those units, Scheffler found them to contain an average of about 164 members (range: 40 to 600), all of whom claimed rights of varying weight in the estate.

Choice of spouse was governed not by descent-unit membership but by closeness of consanguinity, marriage having been prohibited between first and second cousins.

Most of the descent categories just delineated were segmented; the senior segment in each of them, called the "trunk," was most important in that its senior member, by primogenitural succession, had some privileges and authorities over the unit as a whole. The remaining segments, however, were not arranged in any comprehensive hierarchical order.

It should be emphasized that all of the units just discussed were categories, and overlapping ones at that. Every person belonged to (in Choiseulese, "kept" or "looked after") two or more of these units, but in most cases was identified principally with only one, which in the case of most men was the one on whose estate they resided. Because most marriages were virilocal (not, however, by hard and fast rule), women usually resided away from their natal homes and, except for some of them, at considerable distances from their principal (i.e., their own fathers') estates.

We turn now to Choiseul's residential communities, which consisted of one or more closely contiguous hamlets united under the leadership of a *batu* (a headman). The size of communities ranged between about twenty persons to a hundred and more, and their numbers varied over time, depending upon the fortunes of war and the drawing power of individual headmen. The community was the basic unit for fighting, feast giving, and large-scale exchanging. It was also a religious congregation; each one had one or more tutelary deities and ancestral ghosts at whose shrines the community priest (sometimes but not necessarily its *batu*) offered first fruits and other offerings in return for aid in community enterprises.

The residents of a community were of several recognized types. The most priviliged were the "born of men" members of the descent unit owning the estate in which the community was located. The rights of such persons were primary and strong (i.e., they took an active role in community affairs such as disposition of land use, exchanges with other communities, participation in vengeance actions, and control over the unit's hoard of shell-money heirlooms). Secondary status was ascribed to two classes of persons: those who belonged to the proprietary descent unit by birth but were "born of women," and those attached to the descent unit by adoption or capture. The latters' secondary status obliged them to "keep the peace," which is to say that they had to abide by decisions of primary members and never become obtrusive in community affairs.

All other residents had only contingent rights in a community's properties and affairs; they included the spouses of primary and secondary members, and other affines. And although such persons may have participated fully in community affairs (which as residents they inevitably did), their rights were wholly conditional.

The *batu* of a community exercised his headmanship in several ways. He was primary custodian of its lands and shell-money heirlooms, the ultimate decision-maker in its collective activities (but not necessarily leader in those activities), its representative in dealings with other communities, and the principal link with the community's tutelar spirits. He was usually the senior by primogenitural succession of the community's primary members, but he had to be more than that to exercise the headmanship effectively. That is to say, he had to exhibit the kinds of skills that served to enhance his personal prestige and to maintain the loyalty of followers (e.g., accumulating wealth and using it for feasts and for support-winning loans, mitigating intracommunity strife and maintaining intercommunity alliances, etc.; in other words, by some of the actions that characterized achieved leadership in many other societies in Melanesia). In some communities the ascriptively designated *batu* was capable of fulfilling these expectations; in others he held only titular rights, and active community leadership was exercised by another man who had achieved it in competition with other primary members.

Some Choiseulese estates came to have two or more (autonomous) communities within their borders, and although one of them remained known as original (i.e., the one whose core members were also members of the truncal segment of the estate's ambilineal descent unit), there was no overall correspondence between an estate's several residential divisions in terms of genealogical order of segmentation or of relative political power. For no matter how junior a branch may have been in terms of its core members' genealogical position within its overall ambilineal unit, it could have become, and sometimes was, more powerful politically than any other branch, as a result of demographic vicissitudes and of the leadership of an outstandingly ambitious and successful *batu*. But then again, such intergroup relations were never static for very long. Moreover, the rises (and the falls) in political fortunes of Choiseul's communities were facilitated by the composition of the society's ambilineal units. That is to say, because most individuals had entitlements of some kind in two or more estates, shifts in residence required fewer adjustments (such as adoption or fictive invention) than was the case in many unilineally organized societies, provided, of course, the "hosts" were agreeable to the newcomers' claims. Thus, an ambitious and successful *batu* was able to attract followers from elsewhere with greater ease than could his counterparts in, say, Siuai or Mae Enga. And when his fortunes began to decline, it was easier for his disgruntled followers to move elsewhere.

Next to be considered is the Gilbertese society located on the neighboring islands of Butaritari and Makin. The 2,000 or so inhabitants of these islands' seven and a half square miles of land were divided into eight communities but constituted a single society united by networks of kin ties. The household homesteads constituting the communities were situated in long straggling lines near the shores and consisted of sleeping houses (most of them quite large), cooking places, and separate houses for menstruating females. In addition, each community had its own meetinghouse *(maneaba)* and shelters for its residents' large seagoing canoes. The members of this society distinguished sharply between personal property (e.g., clothing, tools, mats), which was owned and transferred individually, and goods owned jointly. The latter consisted mainly of land, sections of the reef, fishponds, stone fish traps, and large seagoing canoes. Land was further differentiated into homestead areas (usually surrounded by palms and breadfruit trees), taro beds (natural swamps or excavated pits), and forest lands (which contained coconut palms and other useful trees). The ownership of all these nonpersonal goods was vested in common-descent units of different spans and genealogical depths.

An individual (male or female) could transfer his personal property however he chose, but the principal, though not the only, way in which nonpersonal property was transferred was by inheritance; that is all of a parent's rights in such property passed to his (or her) offspring, both male and female, and the latters' to theirs, and so on. Thus, an individual could have owned rights in estates from lines of ascendants spreading bilaterally and reaching back as far as genealogies could be recalled (and substantiated), a very large number of estates indeed. In fact, however, other norms and practices intervened to reduce that number, so that on the average an individual possessed socially recognized rights in only four or five estates and relatively unrestricted rights in only one or two.

In specific instances the set of co-owners (the corporation) most directly and actively identified with any estate was one composed of a set of siblings (i.e., the previous owners' own offspring). This was true especially of the homestead where the owner had resided and of the taro pits he had cultivated. Other consanguines (say, the siblings and siblings' offspring of the previous owner) retained some rights in those properties, but of much less weight than those of the offspring themselves (e.g., only reversionary rights in the taro beds). And in the case of a homestead, the society's rule against marrying a close consanguine meant that for most marriages one of the spouses had to change residence. And although a sibling who had moved away continued to have a claim to the resources of his (more usually, her) natal homestead, his own children's claims to it were considerably weaker. Thus, in time the claims upon an estate by its absentee owners became weak to the point of extinction (in the meantime, however, they had acquired or retained viable claims in other estates). Moreover, the claims of an absentee were further weakened when he or she became less active in contributing his share of objects and services to the unit's communal activities (i.e., membership was defined in duties as well as rights). In fact, this disaffiliation was socially formalized in one decisive step: namely, when the absentee member ceased contributing to the food, etc., regularly offered by the unit to the community's headman or higher-level chief, and when he came to be represented by the headman of a different corporation in the community council (of which more will be said later).

The women of this society changed residence more often than men, due, partly, to the circumstance that daughters tended to receive smaller shares of a parent's estate-rights than sons. Thus, although the descent-unit corporations were ideally ambilineal in composition, it was the core of agnates that occupied the corporation's traditional homestead, its *kaainga,* that had the strongest claims to its resources and made most use of them.

Mention was made earlier of a corporation's headman. That official (called "speaker" or "arranger" or "eldest") was in most cases the oldest male member actually residing on the unit's traditional homestead (oldest in age, even if not in genealogical level; an exception occurred when the oldest was senile or disinterested in public affairs). The duties of headman were both supervisory and representative: for example, he supervised use of the unit's canoes, forest lands, reefs, etc.; he allotted the contributions required of the unit for food presentations to the community's chief; he mobilized his unit to avenge wrongs committed against a fellow member; and he represented the unit in its dealings with other units and with chiefs. Concerning the latter, representatives of each of a community's homestead corporations met together on occasion in their meetinghouse to plan community-wide fish drives, to settle intracommunity conflicts, and to receive from and send messages to the society's higher-level chiefs.

When the United States Exploring Expedition visited these islands in 1841, the society was divided into two partly overlapping political units, one (the larger) centered on Butaritari, the other on Makin, but each with some subjects on both islands. In both cases the political unit's chief was a direct descendant of one or the other of the two chiefs who had ruled half a century earlier and whose siblings and offspring were credited with having founded all of the chiefly descent units in existence at that and subsequent times. All members of the chiefly descent units were called *toka inaomata* ("free people"), as distinct from the members of commoner descent units, who were called assistants or workers. It is not explained how the two chiefs in 1841 or their chiefly predecessors came to attain that status (plausibly, through a mix of pioneer settlement and warfare), but the social arrangements thereby established remained in operation until well into colonial times. One aspect of those arrangements had to do with relations between the chiefly and commoner descent-unit corporations, the other with relations between all descent-unit corporations and their respective political-unit chiefs.

To begin with, each of the latter headed his own descent-unit corporation, with its own, very extensive, estates and with enough servants, etc., to exploit their resources. Unlike their humbler counterparts, a chief attained office not by virtue of being his unit's oldest male member but by being oldest son of the previous chief and the latter's principal wife.

The authority of a chief doubtless varied with the times and the man, from benign disinterest to despotic intervention, but two aspects of it remained constant: his entitlement to tribute and his right to appoint the headmen of the communities within his domain. Mention has already been made of the tribute, mainly in food, that every descent-unit corporation, both commoner and chiefly, was obliged to render their chief. As for the chief's appointive authority, the person appointed (usually a close kinsman of the chief and in any case a member of a chiefly descent unit) became not only a community's headman but was endowed with a large local estate, along with the services of local residents to exploit it.

In addition to the above, some commoner descent units had more direct relations with some chiefly ones; not all those of either class were so engaged, but there were enough who were to merit our interest.

One such relationship was based on a chief's *fiat:* he simply awarded to a close kinsman or prominent supporter co-proprietorship over one or more commoner estates. In some cases the appointed co-owner resided elsewhere, in others he resided on the awarded estate, and in some instances even in the commoner household itself (where, it seems, an observer would have had difficulty differentiating him from his commoner household mates). In both kinds of arrangements, however, the commoners were required to do most of the productive work.

And now we turn to Polynesia, where ambilineal descent units prevailed in all but three of its fifty or so societies and where they constituted the framework for most political and religious activities as well.

In 1767, when Europeans "discovered" the archipelago that has come to be known as the Society Islands, its ten inhabited islands contained a population of about 35,000, all sharing the same culture, including language, and all constituting a single society. They called themselves *maohi* ("native") but will be called here Tahitians, in reference to their largest island.

Tahitians' residences were concentrated near the coasts. Their households were typically large and dispersed but were socially grouped into neighborhoods, which were in turn combined into (political) communities that I will call districts. On the smaller islands all of their neighborhoods composed a single district, but the larger islands were not thus unified.

Tahitians gave labels to categories of kinfolk sharing ties of common descent. One such was the prefix *'ati,* which served to identify all persons descended, through males or females, or both, from a particular individual (human or spirit), thus *'ati Omai,* the descendants of Omai (in other words, what anthropologists call a cognatic stock). They also had labels for branches of cognatic stocks and for lines of descent *(firi'i feti'i),* but such lines were relevant only to upper-class persons and figured mostly in the genealogical evaluation of an individual's rank. However, although all the above were important ways of classifying persons, they were only categories and not social groups. In the everyday lives of Tahitians the most important of the latter were what I shall label kin-congregations.

Nearly every particular grouping of Tahitians (kinship, occupational, political, etc.) had its own more or less distinctive set of spirit tutelars and a specific place (a *marae,* 'temple') for interacting with them. (Whatever else the members of a group did in common, for example, residing or fishing or fighting together, they also on occasion worshipped together, hence the label congregation.) In this sense every neighborhood was a congregation of relatives, a kin-congregation. Moreover, in keeping with the ties of common descent that obtained among their core members, the tutelar spirits of any kin-congregation usually included one or more ancestral spirits.

Kin-congregation temples varied widely in size, in architecture, and in accessories, but they all included a stone rest for the spirit(s) during the religious service, a fixed place for the principal officiant(s), an altar for offerings, and a space for the worshippers. (The spirits' place ranged in size and form from a single slab to huge platforms or multi-stepped pyramids; the officiants' place consisted usually of one or more basalt uprights.) In addition, each temple had associated with it, more or less exclusively, one or more tracts of clearly demarcated land (and in some cases, adjacent portions of lagoon or sea). And it seems that anyone who was acknowledged by the congregation's leaders to be a fellow member, either by birth from a prior member or by adoption, was entitled to use-rights in the temple-associated territory. Also, any nonmember married to a kin-congregation's member enjoyed use-rights in such territory, rights that continued after the member-spouse's death, provided he or she did not marry and live with a nonmember elsewhere. However, in keeping with the pervasively hierarchic ordering of Tahitian society, the territorial use-rights of a kin-congregation's members were markedly differentiated (e.g., those of an eldest sibling, especially if male, enjoyed precedence over those of younger ones, and those of a head member of a senior line over those of the head of a cadet line).

When in the course of time a neighborhood proliferated, the additional residences built to accommodate the increase were usually located quite widely apart and at some considerable distance from the "parental" ones. This residential movement was usually accompanied (or in some cases preceded) by dispersion of the émigrés' gardens and groves, to which they thus came to acquire distinctive use-rights. After a few generations of this kind of differentiation, the territory of a kin-congregation, like the group itself, would have become segmented into numerous subdivisions, each with its own temple and fairly exclusive land boundaries. In the ordinary course of events, however, the kin-congregation as a whole, represented by the head of its senior subgroup (in effect, the kin-congregation's chief) continued to have residual rights in all of the sub-units' land, rights that were periodically acknowledged by the subunits in the form of first fruits presented to that chief at the ancestral temple, partly for (token) redistribution and partly for offerings to the whole unit's tutelar spirits. Moreover, the chief of the whole unit was entitled to impose a taboo over resources of its (whole) territory from time to time (i.e., a prohibition against, say, eating its coconuts or catching its fish).

In addition to the process of differentiation just described, some kin-congregations underwent dispersion and differentiation through colonial expansion. It sometimes happened that one or more members of a kin-

congregation left the home territory altogether and established a new settlement elsewhere, perhaps by migration into an uninhabited and unclaimed area or by successful conquest. Where that occurred, and if communication with the homeland could be maintained, the colonials
usually continued to acknowledge their ties with the homeland by rendering first fruits to the kin-congregation chief at the ancestral temple.
Moreover, their derivation from and allegiance to the ancestral unit were
concretely symbolized in their own temple, into which was built a "cor-
ner" stone taken from the ancestral temple.

It goes without saying that among the many kin-congregations into
which ancient Tahitian society was divided the potency of the residual
territorial entitlements just mentioned must have varied widely (e.g.,
according to the size and scatter of each one's subunits, the degree of
amity or enmity among its subunits' heads, and the personality of its current senior chief). Nevertheless, the ideological model just summarized
remained available, to be followed or ignored as circumstances or ambitions decreed.

In listing the criteria for membership in a kin-congregation, I mentioned the rights accruing to a member's spouse, the reference having
been to a spouse from elsewhere. It should be noted that in many if not
most marriages, and particularly between persons of the lower social
classes, both spouses were likely to have belonged to the same kin-congregation, although, except for upper-class persons, some of whom married "close-in" to preserve purity of line, most persons were at pains to
avoid marriage with first, second, or even third cousins. In other words,
kin-congregations were not exogamous, and most of them were probably
wide enough in span and localized enough in distribution to permit and
encourage matings between fellow members. When, however, a husband
and wife did belong to different kin-congregations, their progeny acquired entitlements in both. Thus, individuals could, and evidently did,
inherit entitlements in land, etc., in numerous kin-congregations (as was
the case in Makin-Butaritari, just described), but the potency of such
rights depended upon the claimants' ability to validate them genealogically and the uses actually made of them. In most cases, probably, an
individual of middle- or lower-class status maintained effective inherited
rights only in the neighborhood of his or her birth or residence. Some
upper-class, high-ranking individuals made a practice of revisiting the
various neighborhoods in which they possessed entitlements to maintain
them there, but there seems not to have been any formal procedure
whereby a lowlier person could keep his away-from-home claims
"warm."

The second type of territorial unit to be considered, called *fenua* by the
Tahitians, which is here translated as district, consisted of a number of
contiguous neighborhoods under the leadership of a chief (i.e., a head-

man who was under the leadership of no one else). Chieftainship embraced acknowledged and effective command over the goods and services of people, including war making and periodic levies of objects and labor. The comprehensiveness and absoluteness of that command varied not only with the character of the individual chief but also with the strength of the neighborhood headmen under his command. That is to say, some districts were governed totally and despotically and others only partially and with laxity.

There may have been a time, in the early years of first settlement, when each of Tahiti's kin-congregation neighborhoods was politically autonomous (i.e., when the headman of each of them was a chief). By the time of European discovery, however, every one of Tahiti's districts consisted of several neighborhoods, including in most cases subdistrict combinations of them.

A chief's authority over the persons and territories of other kin-congregations in his district may not have been as direct or as priestly or as supernaturally sanctioned as over his own, but at the very least he received tribute, through their own headmen, in the form of food and other goods, and through those headmen was able to impose taboos over their territories. Moreover, each district also had its temple, which on occasion served as a religious center for the district as a whole; in some cases the temple of the chief's own kin-congregation doubled as district temple, in others a separate and distinct district temple was constructed for the purpose.

Two other aspects of Tahitian descent units had to do with kin-Titles and rank.

The Tahitian language contained generic labels for certain kinds of offices (e.g., "fight-leaders," "official-messengers," etc., including several kinds of religious practitioners). In addition, some of the larger and more important neighborhoods contained (owned) one or more offices identified by a particular proper-name label, which may be called a kin-Title. (The word "Title" is capitalized because of its particularity; "kin" is affixed to it because such offices were usually associated with particular family lines and because they normally passed from parent to child.) In the case of some neighborhoods, certain of the generic offices also passed from parent to child, and in some instances the generic office of a whole neighborhood (say, that of official-messenger) came to be known by a particular kin-Title as well (say, "Swift-imparter-of-profound-word"). Moreover, all kin-Titles seem to have carried some specific privileges, and many of them some specific duties as well; but it should be noted that in most cases a kin-Title was associated with a particular family line in a particular neighborhood and not with neighborhoods as wholes.

A kin-Title was a highly valued social asset, conferring prestige upon its incumbent and, by extension, honor upon the kin-congregation with

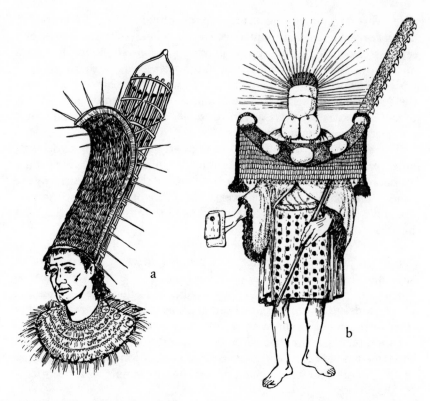

Figure 4.5. Tahiti: *a*, helmet and demi-gorget; *b*, dress of chief mourner

which its family line was associated. Some kin-congregations had none, others one or two, still others a great many. The size of a kin-congregation (hence its resources, fighting strength, level of internal organization, etc.) undoubtedly influenced the number and relative value of the kin-Titles associated with it. Another factor was a kin-congregation's history. Thus, when Europeans first visited Tahiti they came across one kin-congregation (in Vaiari) whose membership had nearly died out but whose several kin-Titles and their associated temples (which dated from an illustrious past) were treated with immense ritual respect but possessed little political influence.

Once created and bestowed, a kin-Title ordinarily devolved upon the incumbent's firstborn (and usually but not always firstborn male) child. In instances where husband and wife each held a kin-Title, their firstborn received both of them. In other words, some individuals came to hold two or more, associated with either the kin-congregation of father or of mother, or of both. (Because kin-congregations were not exogamous, it could happen that an individual's kin-Titles from both father and mother would be associated with the same kin-congregation.)

Another feature of kin-Titles was their social importance relative to each other. All those within each kin-congregation were ranked with each other in terms of ritual rights and duties; and the highest-ranking kin-Titles of any one kin-congregation were also ranked with the highest-ranking ones of all others. The ranking within a kin-congregation tended to be agreed upon and fixed, but ranking of them between separate kin-congregations was subject to disagreement, even to the point of warfare.

Unlike most other Polynesian societies with offices of this kind (and they existed in many of them), those of Tahiti were ceremoniously transferred to their incumbents shortly after the latters' birth; but here a word of caution is required. Although the ritual rights and duties associated with a kin-Title were indeed passed on at that time, the command rights associated with some of them continued to be exercised by the prior incumbent until the successor approached physical maturity. Or, in some cases, the transfer was made so tardily and reluctantly as to lead to enmity and warfare between parent and child.

It was noted earlier that some individuals came to have kin-Titles associated with more than one kin-congregation. When that occurred, the incumbent would usually reside most of the time in the place where his highest-ranking kin-Title was based, but paid visits from time to time to the loci of his other kin-Titles. As mentioned earlier, even non-Titled individuals may have had membership rights in two or more kin-congregations, but the rights of such individuals were of such little social or economic value that they were not often exercised.

Turning to other Polynesian societies, it should be noted that their descent units were continually changing, sometimes branching and segmenting, sometimes fusing, and sometimes dying out. Some changes resulted from numerical increase or decrease, in whole populations or in parts of them. Others were the direct result of particular events (e.g., "colonial" expansion, conflict between and within units, etc.). In no two societies, probably, were the changes wholly alike in manner or in rate. Also, there were differences among societies with respect to the stages at which segmentation became formalized (i.e., at which stage people in general recognized a branch as having a separate collective and corporate existence). Size (i.e., number of members) may have been a factor in some places, as may have been genealogical depth (i.e., generational distance from a common ancestor) or span (range of collaterals), or both, but self-achieved autonomy was perhaps the most common threshold for such recognition, along with the establishment of separate religious worship. However, in some societies, and in different parts of the same society, the process seems to have been so gradual and uneventful as to create ambiguities even for the participants themselves.

As we saw, the segmentation process of Tikopian society was, although gradual, fairly definite and explicit, resulting in two levels:

there were four maximal-unit clans and numerous minimal-level lineages. (Maximal signifies that the descent unit in question was not a segment of a larger one; minimal that it was the lowest-order segment recognized by the society as having a separate existence.) The segmentation
process of Tahitian descent units seems to have been even more clear-cut,
having been explicitly signaled by the consecration of a new temple.
However, little is known about the number and size of Tahitian maximal
descent units, nor about the number of their levels of segmentation,
except that there were more of the latter than in Tikopia.

Regarding other Polynesian societies: they differed widely in number
of maximal descent units and in degree of segmentation. In Mangareva,
for example, all of the descent units were held to be segments of a single
unit, the descendants of an original ancestral settler, which circumstance,
however, did not restrain the segments from warring against each other.
A similar myth obtained on Easter Island and may have been current in
other societies as well, as, for example, in the Tongan archipelago,
where, however, one of the society's nine major descent-unit segments
claimed descent from a Fijian male (but a Tongan female). In some other
places, such as Mangaia, the myths regarding descent-unit beginnings
posited *two* sets of ultimate ancestors, one indigenous and the other
alien-immigrant. (In some versions of this myth, the former were identified with the land and activities associated with it, the immigrants with
the sea.)

Perhaps the best known of all such mythical reconstructions was that
of the New Zealand Maori. According to those myths (which were
accepted by most Europeans to be historically authentic until archaeology and a better understanding of mythical "explanation" belied them),
the Maori's maximal descent units *(iwi)* were united into several larger
units *(waka,* 'canoe') by reason of their respective ancestors having traveled together on one or another of the canoes that allegedly had pioneered settlement on New Zealand during the eleventh century A.D.

Throughout Polynesia descent-unit structure was pyramidal in shape,
so that the whole population of any society was divided into one or more
maximal units, each of which contained two or more levels of segments.
In some societies (e.g., Hawaiian) the all-encompassing nature of these
relationships was obscured by the fortunes of war and the submersion of
lowel-level segments *(ohana)* into larger, bureaucratically organized
political units that were more strictly territorial in nature. Thus, according to Marshall Sahlins, the leading authority on this society, "because of
the large populations involved and the flexibility of the [ramified descent-
unit] structure, genealogical connections may have slipped into the background." Nevertheless, ". . . the ramified structure could in some cases
encompass the entire sociopolitical unit" (1958:162).

The descent-unit system of Samoa presents an obscurity of another kind. Two students of this society have asserted that none of its innumerable small descent units was related to any other outside the village in which each of them was located (i.e., that there were no larger units encompassing localized units into wider genealogical pyramids). These views have, however, been refuted, in my opinion persuasively, by another authority, Derek Freeman, who has asserted that Samoa's lower-level, village-specific descent units were not all interrelated in a single society-wide maximal unit but were nevertheless segments of larger units, including some that had branches in many villages.

EGO-CENTERED KINSHIP

Up to now we have been concerned with membership in ancestor-focused kin units: with categories and interactive groups of persons who based their relationships on (historical or fictive) common descent. We shift now to another perspective, to consider kinship from the viewpoint of the individual. Much less space will be devoted to this perspective, not because it was less important (indeed, for the average Islander the converse was probably true), but for two other reasons. In the first place, descent units are less protean, more palpable, and easier to classify than ego-centered kinship. And second, in most Island societies there was a closer correspondence between descent units and political units than between the latter and ego-centered arrays of kin.

We can best begin by stating that in all Island societies some social importance was attached by its members to relationships with both mother and father (or mother's spouse), as well as relationships traced through each of them, including relationships with *their* siblings and parents and other offspring.

There were a few Island societies in which there were *no* ancestor-focused common-descent kin units, in which the ego-centered arrays were the principal forms used to classify kinsmen for purpose of defining interactive, operational groups. An example of such were the Kiman, the swamp-dwelling people of Frederik Hendrik Island off southwestern New Guinea. In addition to his household and to his community (which contained assortments of kinsmen and affines), the kinship units of most importance to a Kiman were his *jaeentjwe* and his *tjipente*. The former consisted of all of a person's siblings (full, half, and adoptive) and all of the offspring of his parents' *jaeentjwe*. Such kinfolk were expected to assist one another in gardening and canoe making, to exchange food on festive occasions, to support one another in times of crisis, and if of opposite sex to forgo mutual sex and marriage. A person's *tjipente* (literally, "man-tree") was a much larger category, having consisted of both of a person's parents and all of his grandparents and his children, along

with all of their respective *jaeentjwe*. Some members of this category of
kinfolk usually attended a person's feasts and participated in other critical events of his life. The boundaries of membership of a person's set of
tjipente were indefinite; nevertheless, certain specific kinds of behavior
were, ideally, expected from all of them.

In Island societies with ancestor-focused descent units, it goes without
saying that in the course of a person's lifetime, he (or she) had something
to do with kinsmen belonging to units other than his own. Moreover,
there was one feature shared by most descent-unit societies with those
that had none, and that was the part played by all of a person's closer
kinsmen in connection with his major transition rites. Deaths in particular, but in many places marriages as well, brought together the principals'
kinsmen of all types, and even in the most unilineally biased of societies
the principals' non-agnatic or non-uterine kinfolk were usually assigned
specific parts to play.

Affinity

In many Island societies all individuals known to a person were identifi-
able as one or another kind of kinsman, so that marriage between any
two of them served not to create a relationship between them but only to
transform it. Even in the larger societies, whose members were too
numerous and widely dispersed for the nature of all one's kin ties to be
known (or invented extempore), it was possible when circumstances
required to assign one or more specific kinship terms to any pair of individuals on the basis of their known membership in particular descent
units. (For example, if one discovered that a stranger respected the same
totem as oneself, it was concluded that he was a fellow clansman and was
addressed accordingly.) In other words, most Island marriages were
between kinsmen; hence most rules regarding whom one could or could
not marry had to do with kinship.

In a narrow sense the husband and wife, as separate individuals, were
most directly involved in everyday conjugal life, but in all Island societies
one or more larger social units participated in some phases of a marriage
(e.g., in arranging, financing, and formalizing it; in helping to sustain or
dissolve it; and in providing for the widowed spouse). Usually it was the
families or the lineages of the principals that figured in most of these
actions, except for nuptial ceremonies, which in nearly all Island societies
that held them were celebrated by other kinsmen as well.

Concerning the relationships between persons and their affines, it
should first be noted that Island societies differed regarding which of the
kinsmen of a person's spouse were identified as "affines," in terminology
and in expected behavior. In some the relatives classified and treated as

affines were few, having included only the spouse's parents and siblings and the latters' offspring. In many others the category extended to include all members of a spouse's descent unit along with a wide span of his or her bilateral kin and some of the latters' affines as well. On the other hand, there were some beliefs and practices associated with spouses in particular and with affines in general that were fairly widespread. One such was cognitive and psychological, namely the social distance and tension that was engendered between spouses in many societies of Melanesia by beliefs about female pollution. In most other societies, however, there was a disposition for amity between affines. And in many societies having social classes it was the preference that spouses and their respective kinfolk be of equal class status. And finally, another widespread practice was the strict avoidance practiced between a man and his wife's mother.

SOCIAL DISTANCE

Previous sections have listed and exemplified many of the ways by which Islanders categorized and interacted with kinsmen and affines. Other ways, not yet mentioned, had to do more with the distance of a relationship than with its inception through reproduction or marriage. Examples of such practices were numerous and widespread; only one of them will be described, to suggest their kinds of workings.

The Kunimaipa were a mountain-dwelling people of eastern New Guinea. For the individual Kunimaipa the most important way of distinguishing the persons of his social universe was not by affinity or descent-unit affiliation, etc., but by whether they were "pain people" or "pleasure people." I leave it to their ethnographer, Margaret McArthur, to describe this distinction:

> Everybody can cite one and usually two kinship reference terms for the thousand or more men, women and children with whom he comes in contact. From among the hundreds who constitute his (or her) social universe he recognizes a small group who are "his people," his close relatives, with whom he is enjoined to behave in certain ways. He lives with some of them and visits the others from time to time, depending on how far away they are. He helps them in a host of ways. He is ashamed to refuse their requests and tries to oblige if he possibly can. He extends them credit, and ideally he is willing to await their convenience for the return gift. He feels safe from sorcery in their company. If he and they are members of opposing forces in a battle they avoid harming each other, even to the extent of trying to warn against a threatened attack by somebody on their own side. A man should not quarrel with these people or injure them in any way.
>
> He attends their feasts, and whenever he can spare a pig he becomes a supporter at a major ceremony. He gives them pork which they reciprocate. The

generalization is commonly made that a person should not eat any meat from the pigs [his people] raise, but this applies to fewer relatives than do all the other rules. Finally, he should not joke with or tease any of these people, make any mention of sexual matters or have sexual intercourse with them. Because of the restraints and constraints on his behavior towards them they are his "pain people," *kakamari* (*kakamapu,* sing.); *kakam* is the pain of sores and wounds. A man's belly "pains" when he is angry, anxious, or mourning the death of a relative.

All of an unmarried person's cognates together with their spouses are his "pain people." His bilateral kindred forms the core. This means his "pain people" are a category relative to him, not a group in any sense. After marriage the spouse's "pain people" become incorporated [into his own "pain people" category].

"Pain people" are contrasted with "pleasure people," *muzeri* (*muzupu,* sing.); *muz* is the sweet, salty or pleasant taste of [certain] foods. A person's belly becomes *muz,* relaxed or relieved when he recovers from anger, anxiety or grief and when he hears good news. "Pleasure people" include both strangers, for whom no kinship reference term is known, and people not closely related for whom a term can be given. It is said that behavior towards them is permitted to be in all respects the reverse of that towards "pain people."

The correct people to marry are "pleasure people." (1971:158–159)

RELATIONSHIPS BASED ON GENDER AND AGE

Earlier sections have mentioned the many differences that prevailed among Island societies with respect to opposition between males and females, both in peoples' mental attitudes and in their practices, sexual and otherwise. With enough scholarly research it should be possible to arrange all Island societies in a continuum from most opposition to least in this regard, with the Mae Enga near the most extreme and the Tahitians near the other. Instead of undertaking this exercise, however, I will describe how members of two Island societies translated their ideas about sex-gender differences into social groupings.

Having already mentioned some of the many different ways in which Island peoples formalized a person's transition from one "age" to another, I will focus here on some of the types of groupings formed on the basis of a member's "age." In fact, in most societies in which such groupings occurred and were socially important, they were either all male *or* all female as well, the former having been much more widespread and socially important than the latter.

"Clubs" of male age-mates were especially salient in New Hebridean societies. One of the better-known ones was that of the Seniang people of southwestern Malekula.

The Seniang's 30–40 patriclans were divided into lineages, each of whose adult male members formed the core of one or another of the society's small, compactly nucleated communities. Among the several communities identified with each clan, one was "parent," the others "offspring"; the former contained the clan's religious center, where its religious leaders performed rites for the whole membership.

The physical layout of a community reflected the Seniang's view of sexual dichotomy, as conceptualized in opposition between *ileo* and *igah* (i.e., maleness and femaleness). Things that are *igah* were feared by men because they destroyed the *ileo* appertaining to males and the latters' ritual objects and practices. There may have been some connection between *igah* and menstrual blood (which Seniang men considered disgusting, though not especially fear-inspiring); on the other hand, the quality of *igah,* far from serving to degrade women, actually conferred a kind of power and prestige upon them, as its intensity increased. (In this connection, Seniang males also possessed some *igah* until puberty, when maturation rites served to replace it with *ileo.*)

Returning to community layout: each one was divided by a fence into two parts. In the *igah* part were the dwellings; females spent all their time there when not in the gardens. In the other part were the village dancing ground, the large slit-gongs, and the men's house, the *amel.* Although the whole of this part was *ileo,* the intensity of that quality increased with distance from the dividing fence; the most *ileo* places of all were the *amel* and, even more so, a dense patch of bush behind it, where the most secret of men's rites took place. Ordinarily all of the fenced-off part of the community was restricted to men (including initiated boys); on some secular occasions females were allowed within it, but only in the less *ileo* area between fence and gongs. And when men engaged in more profound rituals the height of the fence was raised to the extent that women could not see over it. But, although men spent most of their nonworking daylight hours in their *ileo* part of the community, they usually returned at nightfall to their dwellings in the *igah* part to sleep.

Like many other peoples of Melanesia, the Seniang attached high social value to possessing wealth, especially in the form of boars' tusks. This attitude, combined with their *ileo-igah* concepts, was unequivocally manifested in their institution of graded clubs, of which there were two for men and one for women in every community, and in which progress up the grades was accompanied by increasing *ileo* or *igah,* respectively. Each of these clubs consisted of a number of named grades that could be entered in set sequence by payments to the current members of those grades. And although progress up the grades correlated roughly with increasing age, it depended actually on ability to pay the entry fees.

One of the males' clubs was called Nimangki, the other Nalawan. The rites, etc., of the former were more public and secular, those of the latter more secret and religious in flavor. And although a dead man's highest position in Nimangki defined how his corpse should be decorated, his position in Nalawan determined the whole course of his death rites. Also, some of the ritual objects and insignia of Nalawan were more hidden and inviolate than any of the Nimangki ones, and the seclusion that accompanied entry into one of the higher Nalawan grades lasted a whole year (i.e., much longer than usual), during which time the candidate was regarded and treated as if he were once more a small child.

Nimangki contained some thirty-two grades, entered more or less in sequence, Nalawan seventeen to twenty-three, and in each club the grades were classified into larger categories, of high or low. The more public Nimangki was housed in the *amel*, where each grade had its own section, arranged sequentially from front to back (i.e., from least *ileo* to most); the most *ileo* place of the more secret Nalawan was in the clump of bushes behind the *amel*, which only members of its highest grade could safely visit. Each grade of both clubs had its name, gong signal, protective image, etc., along with special ornaments, insignia, and titles (a man's club title superceded his personal name in daily life). In addition, each grade had its own and in some respects distinctive initiation rites.

As noted, entry into each grade had to be purchased; the most important and costliest item of payment was a boar whose tusks had reached a certain stage of growth. (Sows were eaten only by women and were excluded from all matters of concern to men.) To produce the desired kind of tusk, the two upper canine teeth of an animal were knocked out while it was still young. After that, the lower ones, having nothing to bite against, grew even longer until they curved around and pierced the lower jaw, thereby forming a complete circle and, if left to grow, part or all of another one. The value of the boar increased correspondingly, so that a double-circle boar could buy entry into the highest club grades.

All Seniang males became members of both clubs after they had passed from childhood status *(imbamp)* by means of a general initiation rite, which included seclusion in the *amel* and penis incision. With every advance a man became more *ileo* and hence more prestigious. In the words of their ethnographer, Bernard Deacon: "It would I think be true to say that there is no chieftainship. Authority is vested in the higher [club grades]. . . . It may be noted . . . that a man may occupy a high Nimangki rank because his father, a rich and powerful man, paid for his entrance to the ranks while he was yet a boy" (1934:48).

Thus, a Seniang man had a double reason for acquiring wealth, especially pigs, both for his own social advantage and for that of his sons.

The Seniang women's clubs, the *Lapas,* also contained several grades, whose rites and paraphernalia were similar to those of men's in several respects, including entry by purchase. To qualify for membership a girl also had to undergo an initiation comparable to a boy's, but by having her two upper incisor teeth knocked out. And with advance up the grades a woman became more and more *igah.*

The ceremonies of the *Lapas* took place in a house far away from the dwellings and *amel*. In it were kept ritual objects of such *igah* potency that they could neutralize or destroy the *ileo* and even bring about the death of any man approaching too close: "Even if he were a man of the highest *Nimangki* rank and possessed of a great degree of *ileo* all this would pass from him and he would become 'like a child'. . . . He would lose his . . . rank and title, and men would call him by his personal name; he would be treated with ridicule, contempt, or pity until he collected sufficient wealth of pigs to buy back his former status" (Deacon 1934:479–480).

In New Guinea, the Fore, a people of the eastern New Guinea Highlands, resembled other Highland peoples in their subsistence economy, their (patrilineal) clan organization, and in their emphasis on male-female opposition. They also stressed relationships based on similar age, especially of males.

The Fore word for groups of male coevals was *nagaiya,* which also meant "twins." Males became *nagaiya* in either one of two ways: if they were initiated together or if they were born at about the same time (i.e., of women whose periods of seclusion in the same childbirth hut had overlapped in time). The relationship was extended to all other boys of other hamlets of the same community who were initiated more or less simultaneously. The relationship, which was reinforced but not superceded by close kinship ties, was expressed in a number of ways: by mutual support both in everyday affairs and in times of public crisis, by mutual support in domestic crises, (e.g., if a man's wife struck him during an argument, his *nagaiya* would force her to pay a fine), and by sharing one another's dangers from pollution by their wives (e.g., when a man's wife first menstruated all of his *nagaiya* joined him in foregoing the eating of certain food delicacies). Also, when a man died his *nagaiya* was duty-bound to revenge him and became a prime candidate (along with the deceased's brother) to inherit his widow.

Some Fore women also joined together as *nagaiya,* and under the same circumstances as men. However, because of their absorption in domestic duties, and because of the scattering of childhood partners as a result of virilocal residence after marriage, such partnerships did not actively survive.

PARTNERSHIPS OF OTHER TYPES

The Wedau people of southeastern New Guinea institutionalized a type of relationship that though similar to the one based on coevality contained features of other kinds. I refer here to their *eriam* relationship between men, wherein each partner had sexual access to the other's wives. The relationship between a man and his *eriam*'s wife was conjugal in other ways as well (e.g., a woman mourned the death of her husband's *eriam* as strictly as she would have mourned her husband's). It was possible for men to dissolve their existing *eriam* relationships and to inaugurate new ones, but more commonly the relationship was inherited from *eriam* fathers to their sons.

Institutionalized partnerships somewhat similar to *eriam* were widespread in Melanesia, as, for example, the *taovu* of the northern Solomons and the *kula* of the Trobriands, both described earlier. Despite their differences, they were all alike in their commitment to amicable interaction outside the narrowing bounds of kinship and membership in different political units.

CULTS

Many of the social units already described in this chapter had, along with their secular features, others that were explicitly religious (e.g., the ancestor worship connected with descent units, the involvement of spirits in men's clubs). In addition there were social units in several Island societies that were primarily religious in focus—so much so that they warrant the label of cult. For one example of this type of social unit we can do no better than turn to the Tolai people of northeastern New Britain, whose most notable cult, the *dukduk* or *tubuan,* has been a subject of anthropological interest for a century and more. Notwithstanding that interest, many features of the cult remain obscure, partly as result of some observers' incomplete knowledge or personal biases, but also because of changes in the cult itself during a century of intensive colonialism. The most concise description of the cult's focal activities is provided by Peter Sack:

> Each of the *dukduk* societies was centred around a named female mask, the *tubuan,* which was owned by one particular individual. At intervals the *tubuan* was said to give birth to one or more male masks, the *dukduk*. With the birth of the *dukduk* a festive season began. New members were initiated into the society at its secret meeting place, the *tariau.* Dancers, wearing the conical *tubuan* and *dukduk* masks, their bodies hidden by cloaks of leaves, made public appearances. After two to six weeks the *dukduk* died; only the *tubuan* remained to bear new *dukduk* when the time had come. (1972:96)

The masks consisted of barkcloth, variously painted and decorated, stretched over conical frames of light wood. One of the principal cult mysteries lay in the construction of the masks, a secret that was revealed to initiates, along with the true nature of the bizarre voice sound made by

Figure 4.6. New Britain, *tubuan* mask

the mask wearers when parading in public. It is not clear whether the masks were supposed to *represent* spirits, to *be* spirits, or to be *like* spirits; in any case, although they were supposed to disguise their wearers before the uninitiated, some observers stated that only small children were ignorant of the latters' true identities.

The geographic distribution of the cult and the composition of its membership are also obscure. There were undoubtedly many local, community, chapters of it, but whether there was one or more per community is not clear. And although only males were admitted to membership, it is uncertain whether *all* of a community's postchildhood males actually joined. Those who did, however, had to undergo three separate initiation rites. The first took place around the time of puberty but could occur earlier, for example, for the son or sister's son of a wealthy man (the Tolai had matrilineal descent units). Because each initiation required a large fee in shell money, the second and third stages were in some cases delayed for several years. Unlike initiation rites in many other societies in Melanesia, the *dukduk* novices underwent only playful hazing and a very brief seclusion. And instead of suffering deprivation, their initiations were accompanied by sumptuous feasting for themselves and all other members, which in fact seems to have characterized most other proceedings of the cult as well.

In addition to initiating new members and manufacturing masks (and feasting richly on any and all cult occasions), the members of the cult appeared now and then in public during the *dukduks'* annual period of regeneration, some of them in masks. During such appearances they did at least three things vis-à-vis nonmembers: they doubtless provided an exciting and entertaining spectacle; they hazed and possibly hurt and frightened some spectators; and they collected shell money from all, both universally (according to general practice) and by more direct demand upon a few.

The leader in all this was the wearer (the owner) of the chapter's *tubuan* mask (or masks?; it is not clear that each chapter had only one). In any case, *tubuan* owners were very influential and usually very wealthy men. Some of them obtained their masks by inheritance, others by purchase (at a very high price, which, however, was in most cases eventually recouped many times over). A chapter's *tubuan* owner was expected to organize and supervise its activities. In addition he was expected to "raise the *tubuan*" on public occasions throughout the year (e.g., for dances, memorial services, etc.), presumably to maintain it and the cult itself in viable states. In return for these services he was handsomely recompensed, for not only was he paid directly for "raising" the *tubuan* (both by the sponsorship of dances, memorial services, etc., and by the appreciative audiences), but he received a lion's share of the money collected by the chapter on such occasions. And that was not all a *tubuan* owner gained.

Because of the social influence (or spirit-backed authority? or both?) possessed by a *tubuan* owner, he was called upon now and then to protect his neighbors' goods (e.g., gardens, groves, etc.), which he did by placing a taboo on them, in return for a fee. And more significantly, he was empowered to collect fines not only from cult members (e.g., for breaking cult rules) but from nonmembers as well (e.g., for trespassing on the cult meeting place, for speaking disrespectfully to cult members, and, according to some observers, for theft, incest, adultery, and lying). Clearly, owning a *tubuan* was a very profitable enterprise, but what other functions did the cult have?

According to some observers, the cult served as the Tolai's most important, some say their only, agency of social control, the *tubuan* owner having been the closest approximation to a chief, the only official with enough authority to maintain community-wide law and order, so long, that is, as he kept his greed for shell money and social power within bounds. For, if he became extortionate and despotic, the older members of his cult chapter secured help from *tubuan* owners of other chapters to bring him into line.

In contrast to this judgment about an owner and his motives, another observer, Richard Salisbury, characterized those of 1961 as being: "not only hard-headed businessmen but also conscientious theologians who are concerned about the inward and spiritual meanings of the outward and visible ceremonies which they organize" (1970:301). The nature of those inward and spiritual meanings is, however, not explained.

One other aspect of the cult worth noting is its society-wide distribution. Earlier observers wrote not only of cooperation among *tubuan* owners of different Tolai communities but also of interchapter gatherings. And although this doubtless betokened a kind of society-wide "freemasonry" and hence a check on warfare, it is not reported that it actually had that effect.

Mask-using cults similar to *dukduk* were present in many societies of New Britain, New Ireland, and some smaller nearby islands. Indeed some of their similarities were so close as to indicate historical connections among them.

For another, markedly different, kind of cult we turn again to Tahiti.

It was a characteristic feature of Tahitian society that nearly every social unit of whatever type (kin-based, occupational, territorial, etc.) was at the same time a religious congregation. But there were some social units made up of persons whose only, or most notable, common attribute was their homage to a particular spirit. One such unit was the Arioi, whose members were divided into local chapters that were distributed throughout the archipelago, one to almost every political district. The principal activity of the Arioi was worship of the god 'Oro. 'Oro was also the primary tutelary of the dynasties of upper-class persons, the Ari'i, who claimed derivation from Opoa, in Ra'iatea, but because of that god's supposed efficacy in warfare, he was the focus of widespread supplication by other leaders as well. In fact, reverence for 'Oro had become during the eighteenth century so extensive and so paramount that it attained the character of monolatry (i.e., belief in the existence of several gods but worship mainly of one of them).

For its leaders, the Arioi cult was a full-time and in some cases a lifelong vocation; the facts are not clear in this matter but it seems that most other members spent up to several weeks of each year in cult activities and the rest of their time at home in ordinary pursuits.

Those activities consisted mostly in traveling about from place to place, including island to island, and performing ceremonies and entertainments in exchange for lavish hospitality and within the context, mainly, of 'Oro worship. In some cases a single chapter went on tour by itself; more usually the chapters of several neighboring districts assembled and traveled together. Before arriving at some place, usually at a host chief's residence, they dressed in their distinctive costumes and approached their destination (most often in canoes) with great clamor, proceeded to the temple (one dedicated to 'Oro, if nearby), paid their respects to their tutelary, and then settled down to a few days of dancing, theater performing, feasting, and (according to some European observers) sampling the sexual services of their hostesses and hosts (there having been female Arioi as well as male). Although many types of dancing and theater of the Tahitians contained sexual allusion, those performed by the Arioi seem to have been especially explicit in this regard. In addition, some of their plays were farcical satires containing biting social critique, including mockery of the characters of their principal hosts, a remarkable license in this society, where acts of lese majesty were at most times sternly punished. A week-long visit by a crowd of Arioi clearly was a drain on the host community's food supplies and perhaps a strain on many marital relationships as well, but at the same time such visits were regarded by many in the host communities as pleasurable breaks in their ordinary day-to-day routines.

Because of the emphasis upon sexuality in many of their performances, the sexual license that attended their tours, and the promiscuity that obtained among the Arioi themselves, some writers have characterized the institution as a fertility cult, a grandiose rite of sympathetic magic designed to encourage fertility both of humans and of supplies of food. Be that as it may, the cult did also serve to curb warfare somewhat, fighting having been interdicted at any place where Arioi performances were taking place; and when on tour the Arioi themselves were immune to attack. And although the cult's principal tutelar was the war god 'Oro, the aspect of the latter specifically worshipped by the Arioi was " 'Oro-of-the-laid-down-spear"; in other words, the war-ending, peacemaking aspect of the god. (In Tahiti, as well as in some other Polynesian societies, every high-god spirit had several functionally different personalities.)

There are no credible head counts of Arioi members, but during the middle eighteenth century there were certainly hundreds and possibly thousands of them, and males outnumbered female members by about five to one. Nearly every district had its own chapter, headed by a Master, whose office was distinctively named. Three types of members were distinguished: active, parentaged, and retired, along with two or three categories of persons who regularly assisted the members in their activities. The distinction between active and other members was based on the fundamental requirement that full participation in the cult's activities was dependent upon a person's having no living offspring. Constraints were, however, not placed on copulation: far from it; in fact, active Arioi were notoriously avid and promiscuous, among themselves and with nonmembers. The rule was against allowing a member's progeny to survive, which was conformed to by means of abortion and infanticide. (Whatever may have been the basic reason, or rationale, for this rule, it had the practical effect of enabling members to carry out their cult activities free of family responsibilities.) If, then, an active member bore or sired a child that for some reason happened to survive, the guilty parent (now called parentaged) was thereby reduced in status and forbidden full participation in cult activities. The status of retiree, on the other hand, was entirely honorable; it was reserved for members who had spent years in active membership and then, upon reaching "middle" age, had deliberately dropped out of touring, etc., and had married and settled down to domesticity.

Active members were divided into seven or eight grades (observers differed about the number), from Novice to Black-leg. In most cases an individual became a Novice by application: he (or she) attended a cult performance and in a state of spirit-possession (presumably by 'Oro himself, who thereby selected the applicant for membership) proceeded to dance and sing along with the performing members. If the applicant's dancing, etc., revealed sufficient promise, and (most crucial) if he (or she) was physically well-formed and unblemished, he was invited by the chapter's Master to join. (Physical perfection was a hallmark of Arioihood, along with such other aspects of youthfulness as skill and ardor in dancing, singing, and sex, and freedom from the burdens of parenthood.) At the end of the period of novitiate the Novices were tested in dancing, etc., and either accepted or rejected for membership. After that, members were promoted to higher grades according to progress revealed in Arioi skills (including, according to some observers, deepening knowledge of unspecified cult secrets). Advance up the grades was marked by changes in costume and by different designs and body placements of tatoos. Thus, the lowest-grade member wore a headdress of colored leaves, while the highest-grade member (the Black-leg, a status achieved by very few) wore a red-dyed barkcloth loin-girdle and was tatooed solidly from foot to groin (in addition to all of the other torso and arm tatoo marks acquired in the intervening grades). As is to be expected, rise in grade level was accompanied by increases in privileges, including command over the services of lower-grade members.

As previously mentioned, each local chapter was headed by a Master (and in many cases by a Mistress as well), both of these having been appointed to their offices by the local district chief and from the chapter's active membership. In addition, offices of Master of the separate chapters were ranked in terms of ceremonial precedence, etc., for those not infrequent occasions when two or more chapters joined together on tour; not surprisingly, the highest-graded office was that of Master of the chapter at Opoa, where the cult was believed to have originated. As for the general membership, when they were not busy trying to kill one another as citizens of separate and frequently warring political districts, all Arioi were supposed to behave towards one another amicably and hospitably. To act otherwise was grounds for expulsion.

RELATIONSHIPS BASED ON EXPERTISE

The types of expertise that were held in high esteem by Islanders differed from society to society, as the following résumés indicate.

Gardening

In view of the relatively large amounts of time devoted to gardening in most Island societies and of the importance attached to garden produce (for everyday consumption, for feasts, for exchanging, etc.), it may be surprising to learn that expertise in gardening was highly rewarded, socially, in only a few.

Consider the Trobriands, where gardening was pursued enthusiastically and meticulously and where the produce was exhibited with great satisfaction and pride. According to the ethnographer Bronislaw Malinowski, men proficient in gardening were singled out as "good gardener" *(tokwaybagula):* "one of the proudest titles which a Trobriander can enjoy," but one (it should be added) far, far less "proud" than that held by a successful participant in *kula* exchanges and even less influential than that of an official garden magician.

Or consider the New Guinea Kiman of Frederik Hendrik Island. To these swamp-dwellers gardening was a very arduous and exacting activity, and reputation as a good gardener was evidently a man's highest goal, or so one might conclude from the following statement of the ethnographer L. M. Serpenti: "The most frequent motive for holding *ndambu* [a food-exchanging competition], apart from the mortuary ritual, is disparagement of someone's ability as a cultivator. Derogatory remarks of this nature wound the Kiman in their dearest ambition, which is to be respected and appreciated as producers of food" (1965:234). But on reading further, it turns out that the respect earned by a good gardener was due not so much to his expertise in gardening but to his industriousness, in general, his proven ability to work hard enough to fulfill his obligations to his family and community in providing food.

Other examples could be cited to support the same conclusion, namely, that in most cases the productive Island gardener was indeed respected but more for the uses made of his harvest than for his gardening skills. There was, however, at least one society where expertise in gardening led to leadership status. Reference here is to the Abelam, a people who numbered about 30,500 and who occupied some 120 communities between New Guinea's Torricelli Mountains and the Sepik River plains.

Abelam communities were divided into hamlets, in each of whose three or four neighborhoods resided the core members of a separate patriclan. Each hamlet was autonomous in several respects, having had its own plaza, men's cult-house, ceremonial life, and leaders, who were the senior members (in age and in genealogical position) of the local clans and subclans. Individually, these seniors managed the affairs (including land use) of their respective descent units and, acting together, the secular affairs of the hamlet as a whole. In addition, some of them were known as "name-man," which was the society's most respected status and which was applied to individuals who excelled in the growing of "long yams."

The Abelam grew two kinds of yams, a long hairless species and a short hairy species. The latter were grown for food, the former (which could be tended to reach lengths of up to 10 feet) mainly for show. According to the ethnographer Phyllis Kaberry,

> There is a close identification between a man and his finest yam: it is a symbol of his manhood and his industry. Many of the longest yams (five to ten feet in length) are not eaten: they are displayed at harvest, stored, distributed, sorted again and eventually planted, except for a few unsuitable portions which are handed over rather grudgingly to the women for soup (1971:41). . . . Ideally each clan should have its own big man ["name-man," leader] who excels in the growing of long yams and who may or may not be its most senior elder in terms of age. . . . Over a period of years he has established his reputation— one that is acknowledged by members of his hamlet, by the clan of his ceremonial partner, and by the village [community] at large. His own clansmen entrust many of their yams to him, as may also sisters' sons, cross-cousins and affines. He is described as one who has a name: "This name-man, his [yams] are good. When he plants them they are abundant"; or he is one who "has harvested big yams". He has many garden plots and store-houses; he and his wife or wives produce a surplus of food for lavish distribution at feasts. (1971: 51–52)

The "name-man" of a hamlet's founding clan ipso facto became that of the hamlet as a whole, in which position he was known as *kumu-ndu,* that is, "the tip (or growing point) of a yam or tree."

The growing of yams, particularly the giant-sized *alata* species, seems to have provided much scope for the exercise of expertise. Such expertise was honored in other yam-growing Island societies (for example, in Ponape), but Abelam seems to have been the only one where it was an essential component of leadership.

Pig Raising

"Pigs are our hearts." This statement, voiced by the New Guinea Mae Enga, could have been echoed in scores of other societies in Melanesia. For many peoples who raised pigs, they were the principal criteria for estimating wealth, and pork the most highly favored food. Moreover, pigs alive or dead were for such peoples the most valued kinds of items used for celebrating important rituals, for maintaining or validating social relationships, and for acquiring political power. It is, therefore, somewhat surprising to learn, after perusing dozens of ethnographies, that expertise in the raising of pigs (as distinct from accumulating, exchanging, or distributing them) received relatively little public acclaim, nothing approaching, say, that received by the Abelam yam-raising expert. One reason for that may have been the circumstance that pig raising itself required little technical finesse. Hard and constant work was required to keep them fed (and hence domesticated), to protect them from theft, and to prevent them from robbing neighbors' gardens (thereby precipitating conflict), but such work demanded less knowledge and skill than did, say, consistently successful hunting and fishing. Another and perhaps more decisive reason for the scant public praise and deference earned by successful pig raisers was the circumstance that most of them were women, and in most of these societies women were ipso facto ineligible for special deference and public praise.

Hunting

Skill in hunting was publicly respected in several societies in Melanesia (there was little to hunt for in most of Micronesia and Polynesia), but in only a few of them was the repeatedly successful hunter singled out for honor (one example having been the Keraki, of the trans-Fly region of New Guinea). And in none that I know of was success in hunting a route to community leadership. For example, among the New Guinea Baruya, where the cassowary was avidly hunted and its flesh reserved exclusively for males, and where, according to the ethnographer Maurice Godelier, expertise in trapping the bird was dependent upon spirit-possession (by a cassowary spirit!): ". . . the activity does not confer a very great status on its practitioners. It adds to the renown of those who are already great warriors or great shamans by another route, but it is not sufficient to push the individual to the first rank" (1982:26).

Even among the Anggor (Sepik region of New Guinea), where, reported their ethnographer, Peter Huber, the killing of a wild pig constituted the principal kind of event that mobilized community interest and interaction: "Men are never praised for hunting, nor, criticized for not hunting, and the same may be said of hunting successfully" (1980:52).

Fishing

As with hunting, skill in fishing was admired and respected in many Island societies, but in none was fishing expertise prestigious enough to elevate its best practitioners to positions of overall community leadership. Even in the southeastern Solomons, where fishing in general and bonito fishing in particular was a major focus of social and religious activity, belief in the importance of the supernatural ingredient of success in fishing seems to have deflected respect from the technical to the religious aspect of such success.

Arts and Crafts

Accounts of Island cultures are replete with descriptions of the objects made and the services performed by native craftsmen, but few have anything to say about the craftsmen themselves, except to note, for example, that certain of the objects made or services performed were done by men and certain others by women. In addition, some accounts specify how such craftsmen were remunerated, if at all, or note in a general way about the esteem, if any, in which they were held. There is, however, very little recorded information concerning the position of expert craftsmen (or women) in their societies' social hierarchies. One exception to this deficiency is found in the writings of A. A. Gerbrands, who studied the Asmat, a people of southwestern New Guinea, whose wood carvings have become world famous because of their profusion and, in European eyes, their fine artistry. Among this people, we are told, the expert woodcarver occupied one of the society's two highest statuses, the other having been that of the successful headhunter (whose activities were indispensable for a community's spiritual, and hence material, welfare).

Music and Dance

Music and dancing accompanied some public occasions in nearly every Island society. Moreover, the playing of flutes or panpipes or drums was central in the religious rites of many Island peoples. Thus, it is reasonable to conclude that expertise in dancing and music making was admired and emulated nearly everywhere. And so it was; but in no society that I know of was expertise in these skills regarded highly enough to elevate the experts to positions of community-wide authority or influence in matters beyond those special skills.

Eloquence

Men capable of persuasive talk in public gatherings were respected in most Island societies, although the conventional modes of orating varied widely, from measured reticence to vigorous harangue. In this connection, it should be noted that in many societies it was not only permitted but expected that a man would call attention to his own accomplishments (e.g., to his prowess as a warrior, to his largess) in a manner that Europeans would judge to be vaunted boastfulness. On the other hand,

Figure 4.7. New Guinea, flute

in perhaps most Island societies talk alone was not enough, verbal per-
suasiveness having been qualified by the talker's ascribed status or by his
accomplishments in other activities as well. In fact, there were only a few
societies where oratorical eloquence itself was a highly respected skill.
One such was the Duna, of the montane area of eastern New Guinea,
about whom their ethnographer, N. Modjeska, wrote:

> An *anoa hakana* is a "man with talk", a man with knowledge who can express
> himself forcefully, sometimes poetically and melodically, to persuade his hear-
> ers in the frequent moots that continue interminably whenever men gather.
> There are some men to whom "everyone comes to listen" while others "speak
> only a little in small gatherings, but sit and listen when everybody is there". A
> man with nothing to say is an *anoa yao,* a "nothing man", an uninfluential
> man or a *tsiri,* an ignoramus, fool or coward. A "man with talk" is usually also
> a man with real knowledge, sacred, secular, or both." (1982:87–88)

But for a society where eloquence in the service of knowledge was one
of the most honored and influential statuses, we must go to the Iatmul,
whose large nucleated communities were located along a hundred-mile
stretch of the banks of the middle Sepik River. Each community was
politically autonomous and there was much intercommunity fighting,
including head-hunting, which served to enhance the killers' prestige

and, supernaturally, the welfare of their clans. Where the swampy terrain permitted, a community was laid out in two lines of dwellings divided by a large dancing place on which stood men's clubhouses. The latter served not only as ceremonial centers but as places where men met to gossip, to debate, and occasionally to brawl.

"In this community," wrote the ethnographer Gregory Bateson, "there are no steady and dignified chiefs—indeed no formulated chieftainship at all—but instead there is continual emphasis on self-assertion. A man achieves standing in the community by his achievements in war, by sorcery and esoteric knowledge, by shamanism, by wealth, by intrigue, and, to some extent, by age. But in addition to these factors he gains standing by playing to the public eye; and the more standing he has, the more conspicuous will be his behavior. The greatest and most influential men will resort freely either to harsh vituperation or to buffonery when they are in the centre of the stage, and reserve their dignity when they are in the background" (1958:124–125).

Any matter of general interest could be disputed formally in the clubhouse: "The tone of the debates is noisy, angry and, above all, ironical. The speakers work themselves up to a high pitch of superficial excitement, all the time tempering their violence with histrionic gesture and alternating in their tone between harshness and buffoonery. The style of the oratory varies a good deal from speaker to speaker and that of the more admired performers may tend towards the display of erudition or towards violence or to a mixture of these attitudes. On the one hand there are men who carry in their heads between ten and twenty thousand polysyllabic names, men whose erudition in the totemic system is a matter of pride to the whole village; and on the other hand there are speakers who rely for effect upon gesture and tone rather than upon the matter of their discourse" (1958:126).

Fighting

In discussing this topic it is essential to distinguish between the warrior and the war-manager, although some men were both. The former was the man who engaged personally and physically in fighting; the latter was the one who organized, supervised, and sometimes financed it. Our concern here is with the former; that is, with the man who through skill or bravery or ferocity, or even treachery or luck, or various combinations of these, had wounded or killed one or more "enemies" (however those happened to be defined).

This subject can be disposed of in short order, for in most Island societies even the one-time killer was honored, at least for a while. (In fact, in many societies a male did not become a full-fledged adult until he had killed an enemy.) Moreover, in many Island societies the man who made a practice of killing enemies on all possible occasions achieved a high level of prestige, usually accompanied by deference, including some based on fear, because on some occasions, such men were employed to kill not outsiders (i.e., "enemies") but neighbors.

Apart from actual physical fighting, in many societies the temperament that was usually associated with it (general aggressiveness in manner, outspokenness in speech, quickness to anger) was itself much admired, as a mark of proper manhood, at least in young and middle-aged men.

To qualify the foregoing discussion, however, two other points need to be made. The first is that, notwithstanding the admiration that was shown in many societies for the experienced killer and the warrior temperament, few peoples rewarded such individuals with positions of community leadership on the basis of those qualifications alone. In a few societies (such as that of the New Guinea Tairora) men of this type *seized* leadership, but that is a different thing. In most other societies in which warfare was a major concern, it was the war-manager rather than the warrior who was held in highest esteem. The second point to be noted is that in most societies warriorlike temperament was admired only within bounds, and the behavior that typified it was rewarded with community-wide esteem only so long as it was directed towards community enemies. The men unable or unwilling to curb their aggression within their own community were usually curbed by their fellows by one means or another, including private sorcery or consensual, tacitly decreed, "execution."

Bartering

As previous sections have shown, bartering was a major activity in many Island societies, especially in Melanesia. The goods thereby secured were important in several respects: to acquire needed foods, to obtain pigs for feast giving, to secure artifacts for one use or another, to obtain dance complexes, etc. Many of those transactions took place without explicit haggling but did involve maneuvers of less overt and more subtle kinds (in other words, social-relational skills). It may, therefore, be surprising to find so little evidence of native recognition of bartering expertise—of labels for, say, "clever bargainer" or "sharp trader." The absence of such evaluation is understandable when exchanging took place within the context of politically motivated gift-exchanging, but not for transactions in which dissatisfied buyers had no redress.

Accumulating Wealth

Many ethnographies about Island societies, especially about those of Melanesia, contain statements to the effect that wealth itself did not serve to enhance its owner's status, that it had to be distributed in appropriate ways to accomplish that goal. In most cases that conclusion was doubtless correct, but not in all. Moreover, even in most of the former, the wealthy individual received some respect. The respect may have been in many cases tinged with envy or even fear (e.g., in many societies a wealthy man could employ a hired killer or a professional sorcerer to attain his ends), but similar sentiments were often focused on the successful spender (or distributor or manipulator) of wealth as well. In most of those societies there was a tacitly agreed-upon point beyond which the acceptable level of wealth retention became unacceptable hoarding. And in most societies the chronic hoarder was penalized by sanctions that ranged from contempt to murder.

But leaving the "most" aside, let us turn to those societies in which wealth itself was not only socially approved, but in which a threshold between acceptable wealth and hoarding seems not to have prevailed. Certainly, one of the most noteworthy of such societies was Tolai, whose members occupied the northern part of New Britain's Gazelle Peninsula and whose *dukduk-tubuan* cults were described earlier.

The most highly valued objects of the Tolai were *tambu*, the long strings of beadlike discs of shell that they obtained by dangerous canoe voyages to the Nakanai coast some 200 miles to the west. The Tolai used *tambu* in many kinds of exchange, from commercial barter and payment of services to ceremonial gift giving and funeral distributions. They had a price for almost everything, including edible human flesh. The fathom-long strings of *tambu* were often broken up into shorter lengths for small purchases, or were combined into large coils that were placed in the owners' (lineage) storehouses for safekeeping, an event that took place publicly and ceremoniously. It was the goal of every Tolai man to own as much *tambu* as possible. For one thing, it enabled him to purchase desirable things such as food, tools, dance and song compositions (for performance at feasts), entry into the *dukduk* cult, etc. But more important, it enhanced his status both in the present and the Afterworld. For, regarding the Afterworld, when a man died almost all of his accumulated *tambu* was distributed among the mourners to increase the mourning. And regarding the present, a man known to have a large accumulation of *tambu* was labeled *uviana* ("rich man"), and if he were also a matrilineage headman *(lualua)* he became known as a *ngala* ("big man"), the society's highest status, which usually combined other functions, including manager of most large-scale secular affairs. And although a lineage's *lualua* was ideally its senior member, by genealogy, a more junior "rich man" often displaced a senior but less wealthy man as lineage head.

There were many ways for earning *tambu*: by producing and selling consumer goods (at the Tolai's regular markets); by production and sale of more specialized objects and services (e.g., canoes, carvings, songs and dances); but mainly by exercise of entrepreneurial and financial skills, including the organization of *dukduk* ceremonies and of labor parties (from which the manager received most of the pay) and the lending of money (with large returns in interest). Moreover, although a man's tangible store of *tambu* was clearly important, even more important to his total position in Tolai society were the amounts owed to him, both of money and of money-valued services of various kinds.

Another society in which wealth per se was highly valued was Palau, but wealth belonging to descent units and not to individuals.

The 20,000 or so natives of this 125-mile-long archipelago were spread out over a number of islands that contained several different habitats, from atolls to large mountain masses. Social institutions were uniform throughout the archipelago; in fact, the whole populace was organized into two political confederations whose rivalry, including much lethal warfare, never ceased.

Palau society was divided into a large number of individually named, exogamous matriclans, and these were in turn subdivided into named matrilineages, each of which was a land-owning corporation and localized within a single community. The clans of each community were ranked one with the other and distributed correspondingly by village "side." On one side were the clans ranked first, third, fifth, and seventh; on the other those ranked second, fourth, sixth, and so on. This ranking culminated in a council, the body that governed the community (which in many respects was the society's basic political unit). In the large and handsome houses in which these councils convened, there were reserved sitting places for heads of each of the local clans. Those whose clans ranked first, third, and so on, sat on the front side; those ranked second and so on on the back side. In terms of authority it seems clear that the voice of the first-ranked clan representative was most decisive and that of the second-ranked one next. It is also recorded that those two, together with numbers three and four, were the principal voices of authority (the "four parts" of the community) however many clans the community may have contained.

One reason given by the Palauans for the ranking was priority of settlement (which may have been historically accurate, or a favored rationale for legitimizing what had always been or what had come to be by other means). Another possible explanation for the ranking in some cases may have been the victory of one clan over another in feuding (e.g., over disputed land boundaries). A more likely explanation than either, however, lies in the size and number of a clan's membership and in its wealth in native money. The relative number of its able-bodied members served to define a clan's ranking in a number of ways: in producing food for clan purposes, in fighting strength, in vocal support for their headman in his disputes with others, etc. Female members, especially, served to bring money wealth to their clans, through both bride-wealth and prostitution.

But women were not the only source of, or drain on, a clan's wealth; in fact, the large part played by wealth in general and by money in particular in Palau life was matched in no other societies in Micronesia.

The native money used in Palau was in fact not native to Palau itself. It consisted of various kinds of polychrome glass beads similar to those found throughout Malaysia in association with twelfth- to sixteenth-century porcelains and which were probably of Chinese or mainland Southeast Asian origin. How they got to Palau is not known, but they were an established feature of exchange when Europeans first arrived there. Palauans required this money for many purposes, including use as a status symbol, bride-price payments, ceremonies connected with biological and social "birth," payment of fines for violation of numerous kinds of community rules, payments to spirits (via priests) for various kinds of services, war indemnities, payments to validate office taking, and numerous forms of prestige-enhancing ceremonial gift-exchange.

Money was evidently not needed for ordinary subsistence purposes. However, for many social purposes, such as marriage, at least some of it was essential, and for persons wishing to achieve or maintain high social status it was indispensable. Also, the supply of money was very limited and constant; none was "minted" locally, and for a long time in the past little or none had reached Palau from elsewhere. Moreover, what there was of it came in time to be concentrated within a small number of clans, which were mainly the highest-ranking ones. One can only speculate about how that came to be in particular cases, but it is clear how some of the wealthier ones acted to keep it that way; that is not only by waging successful wars or by "renting" out to other communities the sexual services of some of its young women, but by locally focused measures as well, for example (as described by Roland Force): "Through the manipulation of native currency a lower-ranking [clan] could increase its wealth and succeed in upward mobility, but ordinarily such mobility was restricted in degree; for example, if the members of an upper-ranking and wealthy *keblil* [clan] became aware of the fact that a lower-ranking *keblil* possessed a large and valuable piece of Palauan money, they would make plans to secure it. Perhaps they would contrive a situation in which they could levy a fine and take the money. Frequently they would instruct one of their female [clan] members to marry into the [clan] which possessed the money. They would then bargain for the specific piece in the transactions which required the groom's kin to make money payments to the family of the bride. Such tactics made it very difficult for a low-ranking [clan] to amass sufficient wealth to raise itself in the [clan] hierarchy" (1960:51).

Religious Specialists

Virtually every one of the skills discussed above was believed to be in some measure dependent upon supernatural assistance of some kind. In addition, there were in most Island societies experts whose principal or only specialty was to interact with supernatural entities for one or another of a variety of purposes and in one or another of a variety of ways. At one extreme were the holders of religious offices, whose job it was to promote their whole community's welfare; at the other were sorcerers employed by individuals to settle their own personal, and usually intracommunity, scores.

All three types of religious activities distinguished earlier (magic, divining, and priestcraft) were practiced in nearly every Island society, but not to the same degree. Thus, magicians were more ubiquitous and more prominent in most of Melanesia, and priests in Micronesia and Polynesia. But it was only in certain of the large and more complex societies of Polynesia that religious activity, in this case priestcraft, became a nearly full-time occupation. In most Polynesian societies the secular heads of descent units were also their units' head priests, and in a few cases usurpation left a reigning chief with nothing but his priestly role, albeit a very influential priestly role. (The most prominent example of this occurred in eighteenth-century Tonga, where the highest-rank chief lost, through usurpation, much of his secular authority but remained the society's Supreme Priest, its most sacred person.) However, I am not referring here to chiefs who were ipso facto priests, but to priests who occupied positions of high authority in society because of their clerical roles alone, either inherited or achieved. There were some such persons in eighteenth-century Tahiti and it would be surprising if there had been no counterparts in other Polynesian societies.

Managing and Organizing

As exemplified in the earlier sections of this chapter, in those societies containing descent units, seniority in them almost invariably entailed authority over their members. And in societies where such descent units were wide-spanned and politically functional (as in Polynesia and parts of Micronesia), seniority in them usually entailed chieftainship in their communities, and in some cases in supracommunity political units as well. On the other hand, in societies containing no descent units, or descent units of only narrow span (as was the case in most of Melanesia), positions of influence and authority over whole communities were held mostly by experts in one or another locally valued skill, and in most cases by skills that had been achieved, rather than inherited. Moreover, with a few possible exceptions (e.g., the master yam-growers of Abelam, the successful headhunters and wood-carvers of Asmat, the feared bully-killer of Taiora), the kinds of expertise that the natives of Melanesia valued most highly were demonstrated skills in managing people and in organizing and executing large-scale enterprises both locally and abroad.

Such enterprises varied somewhat from place to place; they nearly always included warfare and feast giving, but competitive gift-exchanging and overseas trading also offered unexcelled opportunities for achieving influence and authority in most of the societies of Melanesia. And although wealth (of whatever local kind) was essential in executing such enterprises, that wealth did not necessarily come from the coffers of the organizers themselves. Just as often, it was borrowed for the occasion or consisted of called-in tangible or intangible debts.

Indeed, even in the most rigidly aristocratic societies of Polynesia and Micronesia, some managerial and organizational skills were needed by birth-right chiefs to maintain full measures of authority. There were always chiefly peers or junior kinsmen willing or eager to assume the role by doing away with the incumbent altogether or relegating him to an innocuous priestly role.

"Tribes" and "Chiefs"

To the Europeans who first visited and wrote about Pacific Islanders, "nations" and "kings" were thought to be universal aspects of humanity; or if that humanity were "savage," "tribes" instead of nations and "chiefs" instead of kings. (Although many of the visitors, especially to Polynesia and Micronesia, persisted in their obsession with "nations" and "kings" however "savage" their native hosts were in other respects.) As we have seen, however, the "tribes" the visitors encountered were in most cases minute, seldom exceeding 1,000 members and on the average less than two or three hundred. And as for their "chiefs," the previous sections have, I hope, indicated how circumscribed their authority was in most cases, and how varied were the foundations of that authority. These circumstances did not, of course, deter the European visitors, then and later, from transforming Island polities and leaders into European stereotypes, but that is a story for others to tell.

And now, before concluding this digest of the Islanders' social relationships, a few paragraphs should be devoted to their concepts of social class, which Europeans served to rigidify in some places and in others to abolish or Europeanize.

Social Class

In my résumé of Tikopian descent units, it was noted that all of the society's lineages were separated into two major social strata, or classes, chiefly and commoner, and that differences between them were based on seniority in terms of birth order and had mainly to do with authority—as

Raymond Firth put it, persons of chiefly lineages were more apt to give than to receive orders. In other respects, however, the gulf that separated the Tikopian classes was not wide (e.g., intermarriage took place and the offspring were assigned unambiguously to their father's class). But let us look at Tahitian society, where classes also prevailed but where the gulfs between them were very wide indeed.

Tahitians categorized persons into three social classes: *ari'i, ra'atira*, and *manahune*. These labels have been translated by many writers in as many different ways (e.g., nobility, yeomen, and vassals; chiefs, gentry, and tenants; etc.), but to avoid the inappropriate connotations suggested by such words it will be safer to gloss them in more neutral, layerlike terms, such as upper, middle, and lower, or perhaps better, to use them as is.

Whether Tahitian ideas about social classes developed out of their theories of conception, or vice versa, is of course no longer discoverable, but the two kinds of ideas were complementary. Their ideas about class held that individuals differed in social value by reason of their birth, and the theory about conception provided a biological-*cum*-spiritual basis for such a view. That theory, it will be recalled, proposed that one element in a human embryo was a portion of divinity, something that had devolved from its original ancestral-spirit parents through all the intervening links. The amount (or intensity?) of that divinity diminished somewhat with every successive generation and in order of birth (i.e., a man's, or woman's, first child received more than did subsequent offspring). Moreover, these theories led to two eugenical concepts of considerable social import: first, in the case of parents of different amounts (or intensity) of divinity, the offspring of their mating would contain an amount equal to somewhere in between; and second, in the case of parents of equal amounts, the first (at least) of their offspring would contain not necessarily the sum of the parents' respective divinity but somewhat more than that of either. However, it should be added that these two corollaries of the basic concept were thought about and acted upon only in the cases of individuals believed to contain a relatively large amount (or whatever) of divinity. The Tahitians showed no interest in this aspect of matings between persons with little demonstrable divinity, which, of course, included most of the populace. On the other hand, among those with lots of it great pains were taken to maintain or increase it: negatively, by interdicting copulation between persons of widely different amounts or by destroying (by abortion or infanticide) the products of such matings; and positively, by encouraging marriages between persons possessing lots of it, which leads back to the subject of social class.

The Tahitians' rules for social interaction included many concerning how the members of one class should or should not act towards members of the others. Regrettably (for the tidy-minded ethnographer), individuals did not always follow those rules, and in many reported instances represented themselves to European visitors as being higher in class level than some of their neighbors would concede. But there was one criterion of class membership that was operationally precise (at least for the highest level) and that was, who could marry whom. Unlike Tikopia, where individuals could and often did marry across class lines (although legend had it that that was not always so), most stringent measures were taken in the Society Islands to ensure that no upper-class individual would marry someone of a lower class. Although most Tahitians were married at some time in their lives, such unions tended to be formalized by nuptial ceremonies only in the case of upper- (and possibly middle-) class persons. And in such cases the ceremonies served not only to link the bride and groom together but, more important, to announce acceptance by the families of both of them of the legitimacy of their subsequent offspring. In other words, the Tahitian upper class constituted a caste.

There are indications that middle-class parents prohibited or discouraged their offspring, especially their daughters, from marrying persons of lower class status, but the incidence of such interclass marriages was not reported by the early European visitors (who for the most part focused their interests on persons of "the better class"). Indeed, it is likely that any effort at that time to draw a sharp line between middle and lower levels of society, by marriage or any other criteria, would have failed. Some writers, including some fairly recent ones, have characterized Tahiti's lower-class persons *(manahune)* as having been landless, in contrast to the middle and upper classes; but that view is in my opinion false and based on an incomplete understanding of Tahitian land tenure. There may have been some families who, as result of forced expulsion from their own kin-congregation territory and before adoption or marriage into a new one, possessed no effective claims on any land, but that must have been an unusual and in any case temporary state of affairs.

Most other societies of Polynesia fell somewhere between that of Tikopia and Tahiti with respect to the numbers of their social classes and the imperviousness of the latters' boundaries, with Tongan and Samoan societies approximating Tahiti's in some aspects of stratification and even exceeding it in others. But see how much further the Hawaiians had carried this Polynesia-wide custom of classifying and stratifying people on the basis of birth.

The Hawaiians categorized persons on the basis of birth into three major classes: *ali'i, maka'ainana* ("people that attend the land"), and *kauwa* ("untouchable, outcast, pariah"), but among the *ali'i* ten levels were differentiated. From highest to lowest they were as follows (after Pukui and Elbert 1957):

1(a).   *niaupio,* the offspring of a marriage between brother and sister of highest rank.

1(b).   *pio,* the offspring of uterine *niaupio* siblings.

2. *naha,* the offspring of *niaupio* parents who were not uterine. A person of this level was not quite so sanctified as *niaupio* or *pio* but like them was entitled to the *kapu moe,* the act of prostration obeisance, the ultimate form of ritual deference.
3. *wohi,* an offspring of a *niaupio, pio,* or *naha* father and of a mother of lower *ali'i* grade. Most of the political chiefs of the eighteenth century were of this grade.

And so on, down to:

10. *ali'i maka'ainana,* persons of *ali'i* rank living incognito among and as *maka'ainana.*

Nothing further needs to be said about the *maka'ainana* themselves, the mass of the populace that provided the *ali'i* with much of their material goods and with the manpower for their wars. But the *kauwa* constituted a category of persons, whole families and communities of them, that continues to puzzle students of ancient Hawaii. They lived in isolation from other classes of persons, and, far from possessing any honor-making sanctity, they were believed to defile any *maka'ainana* having contact with them. On the other hand, they performed a valuable service for the *ali'i,* having been used by them as the most appropriate kind of victim for human sacrifice!

The division of persons into social classes went farther in the societies of Polynesia than elsewere in the Islands, but was not limited to them. As we have seen, on Yap it was not unusual for a pair of villages (i.e., its residents) to be ranked vis-à-vis each other. Most such relationships seem to have come about as a result of the head of a land-rich estate having given a portion of it to individuals rendered landless, say, by war or by over-crowding in their own estates. The new village thereby established became a "child" of the donor estate and was thereafter required to repay the gift with various kinds of objects and services. Some of the "child" villages had the status of "servants" to their overlords and others the status of "serfs." Such, it may be recalled, was the relationship between the parties of atoll dwellers who made regular expeditions to Yap and their Yap "landlords." Like other Yapese "serfs," they were forbidden access to their landlords' women and were required to assume postures of respect.

Class stratification also prevailed on Ponape, whose society was stratified into two major social classes, of nobility and commoners, separated by what the Ponapeans themselves called a "valley" *(wau),* an almost impassable gulf. Marriage between the classes did sometimes occur but was discouraged, and the products of such marriages constituted a named intermediate class, more privileged than commoner and less than noble. The privileges of the nobility included choice portions of feast foods, ranked seating places at public gatherings, wider latitude in sexual affairs, more wives, and, in the case of higher-ranking noblemen, virtually preemptive choice of mistresses and wives.

Even in Melanesia, whose peoples as a whole have often been characterized as "egalitarian," some social stratification prevailed, mostly in societies with unilineal descent units of relatively wide span. In some of the latter, the deference, etc., owed to senior members of individual lineages was extended to all members of senior lineages vis-à-vis the junior lineages of a clan. And although such distinctions did not anywhere, to my knowledge, include society-wide rules against interclass marriage (i.e., their classes were not castes), the seeds for such practices were undoubtedly there.

Sources

Descent Units
   Matrilineal Descent Units: Fischer and Fischer 1957; Gladwin and Sarason 1953; Goodenough 1951; Hogbin 1951, 1963; Mitchell 1976; Nash 1974; Oliver 1943.
   Patrilineal Descent Units: Bensa and Rivierre 1982; Douglas 1970, 1972; Doumenge 1974; Firth 1936; Guiart 1956, 1957, 1963, 1966, 1981; Leenhardt 1930, 1937; Meggitt 1965.
   Societies with Two Unilineal Descent Systems: Beaglehole and Beaglehole 1938; Hogbin 1934; Labby 1976; Lawrence and Meggitt 1965; Lingenfelter 1975.
   Ambilineal Descent Units: Cooper 1971; Coppett 1968; Firth 1959; Freeman 1964; Goldman 1970; Hogbin 1939; Holmes 1974; Ivens 1930; Keesing 1970, 1971; Lambert 1966; Maranda and Maranda 1970; Mead 1930b; Oliver 1974; Ross 1973; Russell 1950; Sahlins 1958; Scheffler 1965.

Ego-centered Kinship: Serpenti 1965.

Social Distance: McArthur 1971.

Relationships Based on Gender and Age: Berndt 1962; Deacon 1934; Lindenbaum and Glasse 1968–69.

Cults: Meyer and Parkinson 1895; Oliver 1974; Parkinson 1907; Sack 1972; Salisbury 1970.

Relationships Based on Expertise
   Gardening: Kaberry 1971; Malinowski 1935; Serpenti 1965.
   Pig Raising: Meggitt 1974.
   Hunting: Godelier 1982; Huber 1980.
   Fishing: Ivens 1927.
   Arts and Crafts: Gerbrands 1967, 1978.
   Eloquence: Bateson 1958; Modjeska 1982.
   Fighting: Watson 1971.
   Accumulating Wealth: Barnett 1949; A. L. Epstein 1969; T. S. Epstein 1968; Force 1960; Force and Force 1981; Salisbury 1970.

Social Class: Bascom 1965; Fischer and Fischer 1957; Goldman 1970; Oliver 1974; Pukui and Elbert 1957; Riesenberg 1968.

Conclusion

BECAUSE this book is itself a digest, a summary of a larger work, it would be inapposite to summarize the many diversities emphasized by its descriptive contents. Moreover, it would not be very useful to recapitulate the several ways of thinking or acting common to all Pacific Island peoples, such as household-based subsistence economies and kin-unit ownership of land; such traits occurred among many other nonindustrial peoples elsewhere.

On the other hand, there was one kind of multidimensional culture complex found among some Pacific Islanders that had no parallels elsewhere in the nonindustrial world and that can be judged to be a high cultural achievement by any standard of evaluation. I refer here to the maritime accomplishments of several Pacific Island peoples, particularly of Micronesia and Polynesia: to their skills in building and operating boats and to their invention of systems of information and practice that enabled them to navigate those boats, knowingly, to destinations hundreds of open-sea miles away. No Pacific Island peoples had succeeded in inventing or adopting, say, metallurgy or alphabetic writing or wheeled transport, but when comparing humans' cultural achievements over time, the maritime complexes just mentioned must surely be rated very high.

Bibliography

Akamichi, Tomoya
  1978   The Ecological Aspects of Lau (Solomon Islands) Ethnoichthyology. *Journal of the Polynesian Society* 87:301–326.

Alkire, W. H.
  1965   *Lamotrek Atoll and Inter-island Socioeconomic Ties.* Urbana: University of Illinois Press.
  1970   Systems of Measurement on Woleai Atoll, Caroline Islands. *Anthropos* 65:1–73.
  1977   *An Introduction to the Peoples and Cultures of Micronesia.* 2d ed. Menlo Park, Ca.: Cummings Publishing Co.
  1978   *Coral Islanders.* Arlington Heights, Ill.: AHM Publishing Corporation.

Allen, Jim, J. Golson, and R. Jones, eds.
  1977   *Sunda and Sahul: Prehistoric Studies in Southeast Asia, Melanesia and Australia.* New York: Academic Press.

Allen, M. R.
  1967   *Male Cults and Secret Initiations in Melanesia.* Melbourne: Melbourne University Press.

Anell, Bengt
  1960   Hunting and Trapping Methods in Australia and Oceania. In *Studia Ethnographica Upsaliensia,* vol. 18. Lund: H. Ohlssons Boktryckeri.

Barnett, H. G.
  1949   *Palauan Society.* Eugene: University of Oregon Press.

Barrau, J.
  1958   *Subsistence Agriculture in Melanesia.* Bernice Pauahi Bishop Museum Bulletin 219:1–111.
  1961   *Agriculture in Polynesia and Melanesia.* Bernice Pauahi Bishop Museum Bulletin 223.
  1965   Witnesses of the Past: Notes on Some Food Plants of Oceania. *Ethnology* 3:282–294.

Bascom, W. R.
1965   *Ponape: A Pacific Economy in Transition.* Anthropological Records 22. Berkeley: University of California Press.

Bateson, Gregory
1958   *Naven. A Survey of the Problems Suggested by a Composite Picture of the Culture of a New Guinea Tribe Drawn from Three Points of View.* Stanford: Stanford University Press.

Beaglehole, Ernest and Pearl
1938   *Ethnology of Pukapuka.* Bernice Pauahi Bishop Museum Bulletin 150.

Bellwood, P. S.
1979   *Man's Conquest of the Pacific: The Prehistory of Southeast Asia and Oceania.* New York: Oxford University Press.

Bensa, Alban, and J. C. Rivierre
1982   *Les chemins de l'alliance. L'organisation sociale et tradition orale dans la région de Touhoaire cèmuhî, Nouvelle-Calédonie.* Paris: Selaf.

Berndt, R. M.
1962   *Excess and Restraint: Social Control Among a New Guinea Mountain People.* Chicago: University of Chicago Press.
1964   Warfare in the New Guinea Highlands. *American Anthropologist* 66, pt. 2:183–203.

Blust, R. A.
1980   Early Austronesian Social Organization: The Evidence of Language. *Current Anthropology* 21:205–226.

Brookfield, H. C., and Doreen Hart
1971   *Melanesia: A Geographical Interpretation of an Island World.* London: Methuen & Co.

Brown, George C.
1910   *Melanesians and Polynesians.* London: Macmillan & Co.

Buck, P. H.
1957   *Arts and Crafts of Hawaii.* Bernice Pauahi Bishop Museum Special Publication 45. Reissued, 1964.

Bulmer, Ralph
1968   The Strategies of Hunting in New Guinea. *Oceania* 38:302–318.
1974   Folk Biology in the New Guinea Highlands. *Social Science Information* 13:9–28. Paris: International Social Science Council.

Burrows, E. G., and M. E. Spiro
1953   *An Atoll Culture: Ethnography of Ifaluk in the Central Carolines.* New Haven: Human Relations Area Files Press.

Burton-Bradley, B. G.
1972   Betel-chewing. In *Encyclopaedia of Papua and New Guinea,* 66–67. Melbourne: Melbourne University Press.

Chowning, Ann, and Ward Goodenough
1971   Lakalai Political Organization. In *Politics in New Guinea,* ed. R. Berndt and P. Lawrence, 113–174. Nedlands: University of Western Australia Press.

Clarke, W. C.
1971   *Place and People: An Ecology of a New Guinean Community.* Berkeley: University of California Press.

Clunie, Fergus
1977   *Fijian Weapons and Warfare.* Bulletin of the Fijian Museum 2. Suva.

Cooper, M.
1971   The Economic Context of Shell Money Production in Malaita. *Oceania* 41:266–276.

Coppett, Daniel de
1968   Pour une étude des échanges cérémoniels en Mélanésie. *L'Homme* 8:759–781.

Danielsson, Bengt
1956   *Love in the South Seas.* London: George Allen & Unwin.

Davenport, William
1962   Red Feather Money. *Scientific American* 206:94–104.
1976   Sex in Cross-Cultural Perspective. In *Human Sexuality in Four Perspectives,* ed. F. Beach, 115–163. Baltimore: Johns Hopkins University Press.

Deacon, A. B.
1934   *Malekula: A Vanishing People in the New Hebrides.* London: Routledge & Sons.

Dening, Greg
1962   The Geographical Knowledge of the Polynesians and the Nature of Inter-island Contact. In *Polynesian Navigation: A Symposium on Andrew Sharp's Theory of Accidental Voyages,* ed. J. Golson, 103–153. Polynesian Society Memoir 34. Wellington.
1978   Institutions of Violence in the Marquesas. In *The Changing Pacific: Essays in Honour of H. E. Maude,* ed. Niel Gunson, 134–141. Melbourne: Oxford University Press.

Dixon, R. M. W.
1980   *The Languages of Australia.* Melbourne: Cambridge University Press.

Doran, Edwin, Jr.
1976   Wa, Vinta and Trimaran. In *Pacific Navigation and Voyaging,* ed. B. Finney, 29–46. Polynesian Society Memoir 39. Wellington.

Dornstreich, M. D.
1977   The Ecological Description and Analysis of Tropical Subsistence Patterns: An Example from New Guinea. In *Subsistence and Survival: Rural Ecology in the Pacific,* ed. T. Bayless-Smith and R. Feachem, 245–271. New York: Academic Press.

Douglas, Bronwen
  1970   A Contact History of the Balad People of New Caledonia, 1774–
          1845. *Journal of the Polynesian Society* 79:180–200.
  1972   A History of Culture Contact in North-eastern New Caledonia,
          1774–1845. Ph.D. diss., Australian National University.

Doumenge, Jean-Pierre
  1974   *Paysans mélanésiens en pays Canala, N^{lle}-Calédonie.* Travaux et
          documents de géographie tropicale 17. Talence: University de Bor-
          deaux III.

Dutton, T. E.
  1978   Language and Trade in Central and South-east Papua. *Mankind*
          11:341–353.

Epstein, A. L.
  1969   *Matupit: Land, Politics, and Change Among the Tolai of New Brit-
          ain.* Canberra: Australian National University Press.

Epstein, T. S.
  1968   *Capitalism, Primitive and Modern.* East Lansing: Michigan State
          University Press.

Feil, D. K.
  1980   Symmetry and Complementarity: Patterns of Competition and
          Exchange in the Enga *Tee. Oceania* 51:20–39.

Finney, B. R.
  1967   New Perspectives on Polynesian Voyaging. In *Polynesian Culture His-
          tory.* Bernice Pauahi Bishop Museum Special Publication 56:141–
          166.
  1977   Voyaging Canoes and the Settlement of Polynesia. *Science* 196:1277–
          1285.

Finney, B. R., and J. D. Houston
  1966   *Surfing: The Sport of Hawaiian Kings.* Rutland, Vt.: Charles E.
          Tuttle.

Firth, Raymond
  1936   *We, The Tikopia: A Sociological Study of Kinship in Primitive
          Polynesia.* London: George Allen & Unwin.
  1959   *Economics of the New Zealand Maori.* 2d ed. Wellington: Govern-
          ment Printer.

Fischer, J. L. and A. M.
  1957   *The Eastern Carolines.* New Haven: Behavior Science Monographs.

Flood, J. M.
  1983   *Archaeology of the Dreamtime.* Honolulu: University of Hawaii
          Press.

Force, M. T. and R. W.
  1981   The Persistence of Traditional Exchange Patterns in the Palau Islands,
          Micronesia. In *Papers from a Symposium on Ecological Problems of
          the Traditional Societies of the Pacific Region, 14th Pacific Science*

Congress, ed. R. W. Force and B. Bishop. Honolulu: Pacific Science Association.

Force, R. W.
1960   *Leadership and Culture Change in Palau.* Fieldiana Anthropology 50. Chicago Natural History Museum.

Force, R. W. and M. T.
1972   *Just One House: A Description and Analysis of Kinship in the Palau Islands.* Bernice Pauahi Bishop Museum Bulletin 235.

Ford, C. S.
1945   *A Comparative Study of Human Reproduction.* Yale University Publications in Anthropology 32. New Haven: Yale University Press.

Fortune, R. F.
1932   *Sorcerers of Dobu.* London: Routledge & Sons.

Freeman, J. D.
1964   Some Observations on Kinship and Political Authority in Samoa. *American Anthropologist* 66:553–568.
1983   *Margaret Mead and Samoa: The Making and Unmaking of an Anthropological Myth.* Cambridge: Harvard University Press.

Gerbrands, A. A.
1967   *Wow-ipits: Eight Asmat Woodcarvers of New Guinea.* The Hague: Mouton.
1978   Talania and Nake, Master Carver and Apprentice: Two Woodcarvers from the Kilenge (Western New Britain). In *Art and Society: Studies in Style, Culture and Aesthetics,* ed. M. Greenhalgh and V. Megan, 193–206. New York: St. Martin's Press.

Gladwin, T.
1970   *East is a Big Bird: Navigation and Logic on Puluwat Atoll.* Cambridge: Harvard University Press.

Gladwin, T., and S. Sarason
1953   *Truk: Man in Paradise.* Viking Fund Publications in Anthropology 20. New York: Wenner Gren Foundation.

Godelier, M.
1982   Social Hierarchies Among the Baruya of New Guinea. In *Inequality in New Guinea Highland Societies,* ed. A. Strathern. Cambridge: Cambridge University Press.

Goldman, Irving
1970   *Ancient Polynesian Society.* Chicago: University of Chicago Press.

Goodenough, W. H.
1951   *Property, Kin, and Community on Truk.* Yale University Publications in Anthropology 46. New Haven: Yale University Press.
1953   *Native Astronomy in the Central Carolines.* Philadelphia: University Museum.
1971   The Pageantry of Death in Nakanai. In *Melanesia: Readings on a Culture Area,* ed. L. L. Langness and J. C. Weschler. Scranton: Chandler Publishing Co.

Grace, G. W.
1966   Austronesian Lexicostatistical Classification: A Review Article. *Oceanic Linguistics* 5:13–31.

Green, R. C.
1970   Settlement Pattern Archaeology in Polynesia. In *Studies in Oceanic Culture History,* vol. 1, ed. R. C. Green and M. Kelly, 13–32. Honolulu: Bernice Pauahi Bishop Museum.

Grimble, A. G.
1952   *A Pattern of Islands.* London: John Murray.

Groves, Murray
1972   Hiri. In *Encyclopaedia of Papua and New Guinea,* 523–527. Melbourne: Melbourne University Press.

Guiart, Jean
1956   L'Organisation sociale et coutumière de la population autochtone.. In *L'Agriculture Vivrière Autochtone de la Nouvelle-Calédonie,* ed. J. Barrau and J. Guiart, 19–43. Noumea: South Pacific Commission.
1957   Les modalités de l'organisation dualiste en Nouvelle-Calédonie. *Cahiers internationaux de Sociologie* 22 (n.s. 4): 21–39. Paris.
1963   *Structure de la chefferie en Mélanésie du Sud.* Paris: l'Institut d'Ethnologie, University of Paris.
1966   *Mythologie du masque en Nouvelle-Calédonie.* Publications de la Société des Océanistes 18. Paris.
1981   Données culturelles et structurelles de l'Organisation Traditionelle des Mélanésiens. In *Atlas de la Nouvelle-Calédonie et Dépendances.* Paris: O.R.S.T.O.M.

Haddon, A. C., and J. Hornell
1936–   *Canoes of Oceania.* 3 vols. Bernice Pauahi Bishop Museum Special
38   Publications 27–29.

Handy, E. S. C.
1923   *The Native Culture in the Marquesas.* Bernice Pauahi Bishop Museum Bulletin 9.
1927   *Polynesian Religion.* Bernice Pauahi Bishop Museum Bulletin 34.

Handy, E. S. C. and E. G.
1972   *The Native Planters in Old Hawaii: Their Life, Lore, and Environments.* Bernice Pauahi Bishop Museum Bulletin 233.

Harding, T. G.
1967   *Voyagers of the Vitiaz Strait: A Study of a New Guinea Trade System.* Seattle: University of Washington Press.

Heider, K. G.
1970   *The Dugum Dani: A Papuan Culture in the Highlands of West New Guinea.* Chicago: Aldine Publishing Co.

Herdt, G. H.
1981   *Guardians of the Flutes: Idioms of Masculinity.* New York: McGraw-Hill.

Hogbin, H. I.
1934   *Law and Order in Polynesia.* New York: Harcourt Brace.
1939   *Experiments in Civilization: The Effects of European Culture on a Native Community in the Solomon Islands.* London: Routledge & Sons.
1951   *Transformation Scene.* London: Routledge & Kegan Paul.
1963   *Kinship and Marriage in a New Guinea Village.* London: The Athlone Press.
1964   *A Guadalcanal Society: The Kaoka Speakers.* New York: Holt, Rinehart & Winston.

Holmes, L. D.
1967   The Function of Kava in Modern Samoan Culture. In *Ethnopharmacologic Search for Psychoactive Drugs,* ed. D. H. Efron. Washington, D.C.: U.S. Department of Health, Education and Welfare.
1974   *Samoan Village.* New York: Holt, Rinehart & Winston.

Hornell, James
1970   *Water Transport: Origins and Early Evolution.* Cambridge: Cambridge University Press, 1946. Reprint. Newton Abbot, England: David & Charles.

Howells, W. W.
1973   *The Pacific Islanders.* London: Weidenfeld & Nicolson.

Huber, P. B.
1980   The Anggor Bowman: Ritual and Society in Melanesia. *American Ethnologist* 7:43–57.

Ivens, W. G.
1927   *Melanesians of the Southeast Solomon Islands.* London: Kegan Paul, Trench, Trubner & Co.
1930   *The Island Builders of the Pacific.* London: Seeley, Service & Co.

Jennings, J., ed.
1979   *The Prehistory of Polynesia.* Cambridge: Harvard University Press.

Kaberry, P. M.
1971   Political Organization Among the Northern Abelam. In *Politics in New Guinea,* ed. R. M. Berndt and P. Lawrence, 35–73. Nedlands: University of Western Australia Press.

Kaeppler, Adrienne
1978   Exchange Patterns in Goods and Services: Fiji, Tonga and Samoa. *Mankind* 11:246–252.

Kakare, I.
1976   Motu Motu Sariva: Trading Voyages from the Gulf to Port Moresby. *Oral History* 4:69–91.

Kamakau, Samuel M.
1961   *Ruling Chiefs of Hawaii.* Honolulu: The Kamehameha Schools Press.

Kay, E. A.
1980   *Little Worlds of the Pacific: An Essay on Pacific Basin Biogeography.* Harold L. Lyon Arboretum Lecture No. 9. Honolulu: University of Hawaii.

Keesing, Roger
  1970   Shrines, Ancestors, and Cognatic Descent: The Kwaio and Tallensi.
          American Anthropologist 72:755–775.
  1971   Descent, Residence, and Cultural Codes. In *Anthropology in
          Oceania,* ed. L. R. Hiatt and C. Jayawardena, 121–138. Sydney:
          Angus & Robertson.

Kirch, P. V., and T. S. Dye
  1979   Ethno-Archaeology and the Development of Polynesian Fishing
          Strategies. *Journal of the Polynesian Society* 88:53–76.

Koch, Klaus-Friedrich
  1974   *War and Peace in Jalemo: The Management of Conflict in Highland
          New Guinea.* Cambridge: Harvard University Press.

Labby, David
  1976   *The Demystification of Yap: Dialectics of Culture on a Micronesian
          Island.* Chicago: University of Chicago Press.

Lambert, Bernd
  1966   Ambilineal Descent Groups in the Northern Gilbert Islands. *Ameri-
          can Anthropologist* 68:641–664.

Lawrence, Peter, and M. J. Meggitt, eds.
  1965   *Gods, Ghosts and Men in Melanesia.* Melbourne: Oxford University
          Press.

Leenhardt, Maurice
  1930   *Notes D'Ethnologie Néo-Calédonienne.* Paris: l'Institut d'Ethnologie,
          University of Paris.
  1937   *Gens de la Grande Terre.* Paris: Gallimard.

Lessa, W. A.
  1950   Ulithi and the Outer Native World. *American Anthropologist* 52:
          27–52.
  1966   *Ulithi: A Micronesian Design for Living.* New York: Holt.

Levison, M., R. G. Ward, and J. W. Webb
  1973   *The Settlement of Polynesia: A Computer Simulation.* Minneapolis:
          University of Minnesota Press.

Lewis, David
  1972   *We the Navigators: The Ancient Art of Landfinding in the Pacific.*
          Honolulu: University of Hawaii Press.
  1978   The Pacific Navigators' Debt to the Ancient Seafarers of Asia. In *The
          Changing Pacific: Essays in Honour of H. E. Maude,* ed. Niel Gun-
          son, 46–66. Melbourne: Oxford University Press.

Lindenbaum, S., and R. M. Glasse
  1968–   Fore Age Mates. *Oceania* 39:165–173.
  69

Lingenfelter, S. W.
  1975   *Yap: Political Leadership and Culture Change in an Island Society.*
          Honolulu: University of Hawaii Press.

McArthur, [A.] M.
1971   Men and Spirits in the Kunimaipa Valley. In *Anthropology in Oceania: Essays Presented to Ian Hogbin,* ed. L. R. Hiatt and C. Jayawardena, 155–190. Sydney: Angus & Robertson.
1974   Pigs for the Ancestors: A Review Article. *Oceania* 45:87–123.

Malinowski, B.
1922   *Argonauts of the Western Pacific.* London: Routledge & Kegan Paul.
1932   *The Sexual Life of Savages in Northwestern Melanesia.* 3d ed. London: Routledge & Sons.
1935   *Coral Gardens and their Magic.* 2 vols. London: George Allen & Unwin.

Maranda, P. and E. K.
1970   Le Crâne et L'utérus: deux Theorèmes Nord-Malaitains. In *Échanges et Communications,* ed. J. Pouillon and P. Maranda. The Hague: Mouton.

Marshall, D. S., and R. C. Suggs
1971   *Human Sexual Behavior: Variations in the Ethnographic Spectrum.* New York: Basic Books.

Mead, M.
1930a   Melanesian Middlemen. *Natural History* 30:115–130.
1930b   *Social Organization of Manu'a.* Bernice Pauahi Bishop Museum Bulletin 76.
1938   *The Mountain Arapesh: I. An Importing Culture.* Anthropological Paper 30.3. New York: American Museum of Natural History.

Meggitt, M. J.
1964   Male-female Relationships in the Highlands of Australian New Guinea. *American Anthropologist* 66:204–224.
1965   *The Lineage System of the Mae-Enga of New Guinea.* London: Oliver & Boyd.
1974   'Pigs are our Hearts!': The *Te* Exchange Cycle Among the Mae Enga of New Guinea. *Oceania* 44:165–203.
1977   *Blood is Their Argument: Warfare Among the Mae Enga Tribesmen of the New Guinea Highlands.* Palo Alto, Ca.: Mayfield Publishing Co.

Meggitt, J. J., and R. M. Glasse
1969   *Pigs, Pearlshells, and Women: Marriage in the New Guinea Highlands.* Englewood Cliffs, N.J.: Prentice-Hall.

Métraux, A.
1940   *Ethnology of Easter Island.* Bernice Pauahi Bishop Museum Bulletin 160.

Meyer, A. B., and R. Parkinson
1895   *Schnitzereien und Masken vom Bismarck Archipel und Neu Guinea.* Königliches Ethnographisches Museum zu Dresden Publikation 10.

Mitchell, D. D.
1976   *Land and Agriculture in Nagovisi, Papua New Guinea.* Institute of Applied Social and Economic Research Monograph 3. Boroko.

Modjeska, N.
  1982   Production and Inequality: Perspectives from Central New Guinea.
          In *Inequality in New Guinea Highland Societies,* ed. A. Strathern.
          Cambridge: Cambridge University Press.

Nash, J. M.
  1974   *Matriliny and Modernization: The Nagovisi of South Bougainville.*
          New Guinea Research Bulletin 55. Port Moresby and Canberra.

Oliver, D. L.
  1943   *The* horomorun *Concepts of Southern Bougainville.* Peabody
          Museum Papers, vol. 20, 50–65. Cambridge, Mass.
  1955   *A Solomon Island Society: Kinship and Leadership Among the Siuai
          of Bougainville.* Cambridge: Harvard University Press.
  1961   *The Pacific Islands.* Rev. ed. Cambridge: Harvard University Press.
          Reprint. Honolulu: University Press of Hawaii, 1975.
  1973   *Bougainville: A Personal History.* Honolulu: University Press of
          Hawaii.
  1974   *Ancient Tahitian Society.* 3 vols. Honolulu: University of Hawaii
          Press.
  1989   *Oceania: The Native Cultures of Australia and the Pacific Islands.* 2
          vols. Honolulu: University of Hawaii Press.

Parkinson, R.
  1907   *Dreissig Jahre in der Südsee: Land und Leute, Sitten and Gebräuche
          im Bismarckarchipel und auf den Deutschen Salomoinseln.* Stuttgart:
          Strecker & Schröder.

Patterson, Mary
  1974–   Sorcery and Witchcraft in Melanesia. *Oceania* 45:132–160, 212–
  75   234.

Pawley, Andrew
  1972   On the Internal Relationships of Eastern Oceanic Languages. In
          Studies in Oceanic Culture History, vol. 3, ed. R. C. Green and
          M. Kelly, 1–142. Honolulu: Bernice Pauahi Bishop Museum.

Pawley, Andrew, and R. C. Green
  1973   Dating the Dispersal of the Oceanic Languages. *Oceanic Linguistics*
          12:1–67.

Pospisil, L.
  1958   *Kapauku Papuans and Their Law.* Yale University Publications in
          Anthropology 54. New Haven: Yale University Press. Reprint. 1964.
  1963a   *Kapauku Papuan Economy.* Yale University Publications in Anthro-
          pology 67. New Haven: Yale University Press.
  1963b   *The Kapauku Papuans of West New Guinea.* New York: Holt, Rine-
          hart & Winston.

Powell, H. A.
  1960   Competitive Leadership in Trobriand Political Organization. *Journal
          of the Royal Anthropological Institute* 90:118–145.

1965   Review of *Politics of the Kula Ring,* by J. P. Sing Uberoi. *Man* 65:97–99.

Pukui, M. K., and S. H. Elbert
1957   *Hawaiian-English Dictionary.* Honolulu: University of Hawaii Press.

Rappaport, R. R.
1968   *Pigs For the Ancestors: Ritual in the Ecology of a New Guinea People.* New Haven: Yale University Press.

Reinman, F. M.
1967   *Fishing: An Aspect of Oceanic Economy. An Archaeological Approach.* Fieldiana Anthropology 56, no. 2. Chicago: Field Museum of Natural History.

Riesenberg, S. H.
1968   *The Native Polity of Ponape.* Washington, D.C.: Smithsonian Contributions to Anthropology, 10.
1976   The Organization of Navigational Knowledge on Puluwat. In *Pacific Navigation and Voyaging,* ed. B. R. Finney, 91–128. Polynesian Society Memoir 39.

Ross, H. M.
1973   *Baegu: Social and Ecological Organization in Malaita, Solomon Islands.* Illinois Studies in Anthropology 8. Urbana: University of Illinois Press.
1978   Baegu Markets: Areal Integration and Economic Efficiency in Malaita, Solomon Islands. *Ethnology* 17:119–138.

Russell, T.
1950   The Fataleka of Malaita. *Oceania* 21:1–13.

Sack, P. G.
1972   Dukduk and Law Enforcement. *Oceania* 43:96–103.

Sahlins, M. D.
1958   *Social Stratification in Polynesia.* Seattle: University of Washington Press.
1962   *Moala: Culture and Nature on a Fijian Island.* Ann Arbor: University of Michigan Press.
1972   *Stone Age Economics.* Chicago: Aldine Publishing Co.

Salisbury, R. F.
1970   *Vunamami: Economic Transformations in a Traditional Society.* Berkeley: University of California Press.

Scheffler, H. W.
1965   *Choiseul Island Social Structure.* Berkeley: University of California Press.

Schneider, D. M.
1968   Virgin Birth. *Man* n.s. 3:120–129.

Schwartz, Theodore
1963   Systems of Areal Integration: Some Considerations Based on the Admiralty Islands of Northern Melanesia. *Anthropological Forum* 1:56–97.

Serpenti, L. M.
  1965   *Cultivators in the Swamps: Social Structure and Horticulture in a
          New Guinea Society.* Assen: van Gorcum.
Sharp, Andrew
  1963   *Ancient Voyagers in Polynesia.* Berkeley: University of California
          Press.
Strathern, Andrew
  1969   Finance and Production: Two Strategies in New Guinea Highlands
          Exchange Systems. *Oceania* 40:42–67.
  1971   *The Rope of Moka.* Cambridge: Cambridge University Press.
Thomas, W. L.
  1968   The Pacific Basin: An Introduction. In *Peoples and Cultures of the
          Pacific,* ed. A. P. Vayda, 3–26. Garden City, N.Y.: Natural History
          Press.
Thomson, Basil
  1908   *The Fijians: A Study of the Decay of Custom.* London: William
          Heinemann.
Tippet, A. R.
  1968   *Fijian Material Culture: A Study of Cultural Context, Function, and
          Change.* Bernice Pauahi Bishop Museum Bulletin 232.
Titcomb, M.
  1969   *Dog and Man in the Ancient Pacific.* Bernice Pauahi Bishop Museum
          Special Publication 59.
Townsend, P. K. W.
  1970   Subsistence and Social Organization in a New Guinea Society. Ph.D.
          diss., University of Michigan.
Uberoi, J. P. S.
  1962   *Politics of the Kula Ring: An Analysis of the Findings of Bronislaw
          Malinowski.* Manchester: The University Press.
Valle, Teresa del
  1987   *Culturas Oceánicas Micronesia.* Barcelona: Editorial Anthropos.
Vayda, A. P.
  1960   *Maori Warfare.* Polynesian Society Monograph 2.
Watson, J. B.
  1971   Tairora: The Politics of Despotism in a Small Society. In *Politics in
          New Guinea,* ed. R. M. Berndt and P. Lawrence, 224–275. Ned-
          lands: University of Western Australia Press.
White, J. P., and J. F. O'Connell
  1982   *A Prehistory of Australia, New Guinea and Sahul.* Sydney: Academic
          Press.
Wilkes, Charles
  1845   *Narrative of the United States Exploring Expedition, During the
          Years 1838, 1839, 1840, 1841, 1842.* 5 vols. London and Philadel-
          phia: Wiley & Putnam.

Williams, F. E.
 1936   *Papuans of the Trans-Fly.* Oxford: Clarendon Press.

Williams, Thomas
 1858   *Fiji and the Fijians.* Vol. 1, *The Islands and Their Inhabitants.* London: Alexander Heylin.

Wurm, S. A., ed.
 1975   Papuan Linguistic Prehistory, and Past Language Migrations in the New Guinea Area. In *Pacific Linguistics,* ser. C, no. 38. Canberra: Australian National University.

Yen, D. E.
 1973   The Origins of Oceanic Agriculture. *Archaeology and Physical Anthropology in Oceania* 8:68–85.
 1974   *The Sweet Potato and Oceania.* Bernice Pauahi Bishop Museum Bulletin 236.
 1980   The Southeast Asian Foundations of Oceanic Agriculture: A Reassessment. *Journal de la Société des Océanistes* 36:140–147.

Young, M. W.
 1971   *Fighting With Food: Leadership, Values and Social Control in a Massim Society.* Cambridge: Cambridge University Press.

Zegwaard, G. A.
 1959   Headhunting Practices of the Asmat of West New Guinea. *American Anthropologist* 61:1020–1041.

Index

The principal authors whose writings were used in preparing this digest are listed in the Bibliography and, more specifically, under "Sources" at the end of each chapter. Those listed in the following index include only the ones directly quoted in the text. The index also includes the names of "peoples" specifically named in the text (e.g., Asmat, Mae Enga), but not place names as such except in the cases where a people are generally labeled by their location: for example, the Fijians (the people of the Fiji islands), the Tikopians (the people of the island of Tikopia).

About the Author

DOUGLAS L. OLIVER is emeritus professor of anthropology at Harvard University and the University of Hawaii. Educated at Harvard and the University of Vienna, he has been concerned with the Pacific Islands since 1936. He has carried out field research in New Guinea, the northern Solomons, and the Society Islands and has written more than a dozen books on the islands of the Pacific. He is a Member of the National Academy of Sciences and a Fellow of the American Academy of Arts and Sciences. He and his wife, the Australian anthropologist Margaret McArthur, now live in Honolulu, where they continue writing.